Living with
Coco Chanel

Living with
Coco Chanel

The homes and landscapes
that shaped the designer
Caroline Young

WHITE
LION
PUBLISHING

Contents

Previous spread: Coco
Chanel, by Cecil Beaton,
featured in *Vogue*, 1935.

Gabrielle 'Coco'
Chanel, 1961.

Following spread: From
1910, Paris was the home
of the House of Chanel.

The Country Girl

'I love everything that's up high. The sky, the moon, and I believe in the stars. I was born under the sign of the Lion, like Nostradamus.'

Saumur, Aubazine, Moulins, Royallieu
1883–1908

Gabrielle Chanel kept many facts about her childhood secret. She only offered hints about the poverty and the abandonment she had suffered, of the cloisters and chestnut trees of the Auvergne landscape that formed a backdrop to her early life.

She was born on 19 August 1883, under the Leo star sign. Being superstitious, she chose the lion symbol for many aspects of her life – in her apartment in rue Cambon, Paris, on her creations and as a marker on her headstone in the cemetery of Lausanne. 'I love everything that's up high,' she said. 'The sky, the moon, and I believe in the stars. I was born under the sign of the Lion, like Nostradamus. I'd rather have a touch of the invisible than roast mutton every day.'[1]

While it was known that Chanel was born poor, she obscured the parts of her story of which she was ashamed, instead detailing a softened, fantasy version of her childhood to biographers, only recounting some of the hardships she suffered. Her father Albert Chanel's ancestry is traced to the Cévennes region, a rural area marked by its limestone peaks and ravines, where shepherds tended their flocks, where chestnuts and mulberries were the main harvests and silk farming and weaving – eighteenth-century industries – were still in common practice. Albert's father, Henri-Adrien, was born in Ponteils-et-Brésis, a village built on lush, green, undulating slopes with views over the mountains. The people of the region lived in homes of slate stone with sloping roofs. From the beginning of the nineteenth century, Henri-Adrien's family owned a tavern that was part of a large farmhouse called Mas Chanel, built in 1740, and where generations of Chanels were raised.[2] Henri-Adrien became a market trader, raising nineteen children with his wife Émilie Virginie Angélina. Albert, their eldest son, followed in his father's footsteps as a peddler, selling everything from wine to haberdashery and clothing across rural France.

Albert was a charmer, regularly flirting with village girls. After stopping for the winter in Courpière, in 1881, he seduced Jeanne Devolle, a sixteen-year-old seamstress and the sister of his

Twenty-three-year-old Gabrielle Chanel in 1906.

landlord. When Jeanne discovered she was pregnant, Albert quickly disappeared, but Jeanne's family traced him to a tavern in Aubenas, and told him to take responsibility for Jeanne, who gave birth to a daughter, Julie-Berthe, in September 1882.

The town of Saumur, in the Loire Valley, catered for smart officers of the military cavalry school, all dressed in leather riding boots and high-collared coats. It was here that Gabrielle Chanel was born, in 1883, and where her parents stayed for her first year on 29 rue St Jean. Gabrielle felt that, because she was born in an equestrian town, under the symbol of the lion, she had the dual protection of both horse and lion.[3]

'I was born on a journey,' she told a journalist. 'My father was not there. That poor woman, my mother, had to go looking for him. It's a sad story, and very boring – I've heard it so many times…'[4] She was born in a hospice for the poor, run by nuns, and baptised quickly because she was unwell. She said the nun who took care of her named her Gabrielle Bonheur as a baby, and the registrar, unable to spell the surname, noted it down as 'Chasnel' – the spelling of which is still on the birth certificate.

Albert finally agreed to marry Jeanne in November 1884, after her family paid a dowry. He and Jeanne moved to the market town Issoire, and in 1885 Jeanne gave birth to a son, Alphonse. A third daughter, Antoinette, was born in 1887 in Saintes, and in 1889 Jeanne gave birth to her fifth child, Lucien, in Gueret.

Travelling from town to town, the Chanel children were raised

The Chanel ancestral family home, built in 1740, is located in the remote town of Ponteils-et-Brésis, in the pine-covered mountains of the Cévennes region of France.

around bustling public market places, staying in cheap lodgings in artisan quarters. Trades were predominantly pre-industrial, such as leather and candlemaking, joinery and clothmaking, and Albert bought and sold such goods. He began to specialise in work clothes and undergarments, perhaps made from cheap, flexible jersey fabric.[5]

One of Gabrielle's early memories was playing in a cemetery, creating fairy-tale worlds amongst the weeds and bringing presents for the dead. Other recollections included her father comforting her after nightmares, placing wheat by her bed as a good luck charm. As an adult Chanel kept wheat in her homes, as a symbol of the wealth and prosperity of the harvest.[6]

Chanel also recalled a room covered in red wallpaper. Her mother had taken Gabrielle and her two sisters to the home of an elderly uncle in Issoire, and left in a room on their own, the bored, naughty girls began peeling strips of paper from the wall. 'We placed the stack of chairs on a table and managed to strip away the paper as far as the ceiling: the pleasure was sublime!' she recalled. 'At last, my mother came in; she stood stock still, contemplating the disaster. She didn't say a word to us; in the depths of her despair all she did was weep silently; no reprimand could have had such an effect on me; I ran away, howling with sorrow: we never saw the uncle from Issoire again.'[7]

With the strain of a quick succession of multiple pregnancies, Jeanne suffered from poor health, developing asthma and tuberculosis from living in the cold lodgings. Jeanne's white handkerchiefs were often stained with blood and Gabrielle and her siblings were kept away so as not to catch the illness. Eventually Jeanne succumbed. In February 1895, she was found dead in her bed in the town of Brive-la-Gaillarde. Albert was absent when she died, and unable and unwilling to take on responsibility for the children. He left the two boys with farmers, essentially as free labour, and the girls were delivered to a convent orphanage at the nearby abbey of Aubazine. It is thought that Albert took them there in his horse-drawn cart, or that he left them with his parents, who then took them to Aubazine.[8]

Chanel was twelve years old when she was abandoned, but in her revisionist history she became six, and was left with two strict aunts dressed in black, who were 'good people, but absolutely without tenderness'.[9] It's now known that the aunts of her recollections were the nuns of the convent. Part of Chanel's fabrication of her past lay in her fears at being discovered as 'illegitimate'. She even refused to change the spelling of 'Chasnel' on her birth certificate to avoid the truth of her life in the orphanage coming out.

Chanel recalled arriving at the 'aunts' house in Mont-Dore at dusk, with her father who was in deep mourning for her mother. 'When we get there, we are greeted half-heartedly; they cut the wick of the lamp to see my face more clearly. My aunts have had supper; we haven't; they are surprised that people who have been travelling all day should not have eaten. This disturbs their routine and their household management, but eventually they overcome their harsh, provincial austerity and say reluctantly: "We shall cook you two boiled eggs."'[10]

Aubazine village is situated on a long ridge protected by wooded hills, isolated from main roads and looking out over the Coyroux mountain stream. The village, a collection of little

The orphanage at Aubazine Abbey in Corrèze was home to Chanel from the age of twelve until eighteen.

thick-walled houses with grey-slate gabled roofs, was quite different from the bustle of the market towns, yet its remoteness had attracted its medieval founder.

The monastery at Aubazine had been established by hermit Étienne de Vielzot, who devoted himself to God by living as simply as possible. Following the Rule of St Benedict and the Cistercians, a monastery was built in 1142 for Étienne's disciples. The Romanesque abbey, dedicated to the Virgin Mary, became a resting place for pilgrims on their journey to Santiago de Compostela in northwest Spain. The Cistercian Order encouraged an austere life of manual labour and isolation from the outside world, and each monastery was to be as autonomous as possible. The monastery was donated to the Congregation of the Holy Heart of Mary in the mid-nineteenth century, and an orphanage opened for girls in 1860, the largest in the region.[11]

Linked with vaulted passageways and arches, the monastic buildings surrounded a square cloister with a fountain and

The abbey's cloisters and gardens of lavender would later shape the design of Chanel's villa on the Cote d'Azur.

flowerbeds of lavender. The whitewashed walls of the corridors in the orphanage contrasted with black-painted doors that opened onto large, cold rooms.

It was very bleak in the winter. The girls slept in an unheated dormitory on iron beds, with crucifixes hanging above them, and from the windows they could see out over the chestnut trees, the forests and hills. Breakfast was watery porridge served on rows of tables in the dining halls. The girls studied for six days a week, and in the evenings they practised housekeeping skills, such as hemming bed sheets, vital for a life to be spent in domestic servitude. Sunday mornings were devoted to mass, and in the afternoons the girls often walked to the summit of Coyroux.[12]

When Chanel talked of the cleanliness of her aunts' house, she must surely have been referring to the orphanage. 'If I have a certain preference for order, for comfort, for having things done right, for chests filled with linens that smell good, and gleaming floors, I owe it to my aunts. Living with them gave me that solid substance that is to be found only in the French.' She remembered, in the spring, every chest was emptied and the linens sorted out and cleaned and pressed. 'Now sheets smell of chlorine everywhere; at the Ritz they're changed every day, so that every night I go to sleep in the aroma of chlorine. Life in the country was luxurious.'[13]

The convent at Aubazine offers a glimpse into the creative mind of Chanel. It was from her memories here that she created many of her signature pieces, including her black, white and beige colour scheme. White stood for the clean sheets in old chests, and beige for the natural sandstone and wood. The nuns walked the white corridors in their black and white habits, with the girls in their own black skirt and white blouse uniform. Hundreds of years before, the monks had created a stone mosaic in the long corridor leading to the rooms, which depicted moons, stars and crosses, and these symbols would manifest in Chanel's jewellery collections. The Maltese cross, for example, was first depicted in precious stones in a 1937 white-enamel cuff bracelet, while her first diamond collection, in 1932, used precious jewels to create constellation designs.

Each day the girls padded up and down a stone staircase into the abbey as they made their way from their dormitories to the

The windows at the abbey of Aubazine may have been the inspiration for the double C Chanel logo.

The monochrome simplicity of Chanel's creations was inspired by the nuns' habits and convent uniforms of Aubazine. Black suit with cream blouse, circa 1927, Metropolitan Museum of Art, New York.

abbey for daily prayers. The steps were worn down by centuries of trailing feet. At the bottom was a twelfth-century liturgical oak cupboard considered to be the oldest cupboard in France, and which resembled the architecture of a church.[14]

Light entered the church through deep, arched windows, with grisaille window panes made from colourless glass set into leaded geometric patterns that included Celtic knots. This was the only type of glass permitted by Cistercian churches – coloured patterns were considered too ornate and contrary to the sense of austerity.[15] The young Gabrielle would have gazed upon these windows frequently during her years at the convent. In the abbey there is a sign that demonstrates how these interconnected swirls form a similar shape to the famous Chanel double C logo. Did she remember the shape of these windows when thinking of her branding? Maybe those years of praying in the abbey, the light streaming through the windows, remained imprinted in her mind.

The town of Aubazine,
surrounded by hills and
chestnut-tree woodlands,
was a place chosen by
the abbey's Cistercian
founders for its isolation.

In Chanel's retelling of her childhood story, it was always winter. She romanticised the warm hearth, the bare branches of chestnut trees and snow-covered hills. 'Winters were frightful – winters nowadays aren't what they used to be. I loved winter. I was allowed to stay in the kitchen, and we burned trees in the fireplace. In the country the kitchen is the soul of the house. When people came in, frozen, you filled their pockets with chestnuts, and gave them more when they went out again. Potatoes for the pigs were boiled in a big cast-iron pot hung over the fire.'[16]

The young Gabrielle was fierce and angry. She recognised life's injustices, and resented the nuns for a lack of love. She would say she owed her 'aunts' everything, because they created her inner resolve – starving her of love rather than coddling her. 'It's the mean and nasty aunts who create winners, and give them inferiority complexes, although in my case the result was a superiority complex. Under nastiness looms strength, under pride a taste for success and a passion for grandeur.'

Gabrielle wasn't completely without family – she was allowed to spend holidays with her grandparents. She also formed a close friendship with her youngest aunt Adrienne, the nineteenth of

Moulins around 1900, with the Notre-Dame cathedral in the background, at the time Chanel attended.

Virginie and Henri-Adrien's children, only a few years older than Gabrielle, and more like a sister.

As a teenager, Gabrielle discovered the romantic stories of French writer Pierre Decourcelle, which served to fire up her imagination where there 'was nothing but silk pillows and white-lacquered furniture. I'd have liked to do everything in white lacquer.' After visiting her grandparents she took these stories, essentially newspaper clippings, back to the orphanage, where she supposedly hid them in the loft. 'The catalogues I read gave me wild dreams of spending. I imagined myself wearing a white woollen dress; I wanted a bedroom painted in white gloss, with white curtains. What a contrast this white made with the dark house in which my aunts confined me.'[17]

Clues from the stories she told her biographers help to understand where Chanel's designs came from, and while they may be part fantasy, they serve as an allegory to her life. She admitted that 'Indirectly, it was my Auvergne aunts who imposed their modesty on the beautiful Parisian ladies. Years have gone by, and it is only now that I realise that the austerity of dark shades, the respect for colours borrowed from nature, the almost monastic cut of my summer alpaca wear and of my winter tweed suits, all that puritanism that elegant ladies would go crazy for, came from Mont-Dore.'[18]

Moulins

When the three Chanel sisters each turned eighteen, the nuns arranged a transfer to the Notre-Dame convent in the centre of Moulins, where they would be closer to their grandparents and aunt Adrienne, who lived in Vichy.

The convent school mixed fee-paying students with charity pupils, who received a free place in exchange for work. The private boarders were clothed in claret cashmere, straw boaters, cloaks and new shoes, while the charity schoolgirls wore rough wool pelerines, knitted in the convent's workroom, and second-hand ankle boots donated by the congregation.[19] The girls' duties involved embroidering initials on towels, or sewing crosses onto nightdresses, and while this work made Gabrielle want to 'spit', these skills would prove useful, as it allowed her to earn money to gain the freedom she craved.[20]

Moulins, circa 1900. Chanel worked as a seamstress at H. Desboutins, located in the cobbled, medieval streets around the Jacquemart clock tower.

Moulins was a lively place owing to several military regiments that stayed at the barracks, Quartier Villars, close to the river and the medieval old town. The Tenth Light Horse was the most prestigious, and its moustached, wealthy men wore dashing uniforms of scarlet breeches, pristine white gloves and peaked caps worn at an angle over one ear. Days were spent at the racetrack or flirting at the modern art nouveau pastry shops, and evenings in the music halls, drinking as the chanteuses sang bawdy songs.

The convent's Mother Superior granted Gabrielle permission to work with her aunt Adrienne as a sales assistant at a lingerie shop, the House of Grampayre, on rue de l'Horloge, which offered a direct view along its narrow cobbled street to the clock on Jacquemart tower. The owners, the Desboutins, liked to hire girls from Notre-Dame as they were highly skilled at sewing. They gave the girls a third-floor attic room to share.[21]

By 1904, Gabrielle and Adrienne had moved into a room in the popular, but down-at-heel, street in Moulins, rue du Pont Ginguet. To earn more money, they each took on an extra Sunday job. There was plenty of work for seamstresses in the town, as there were military uniforms and racing clothing to alter and stitch.

Gabrielle was now twenty years old, beautiful and lively. 'I was told I had black eyes,' she said. 'I have an unbelievably long neck. Look how far it extends to the nape. No one has a neck as long as mine, particularly in photographs. I always hold my head high when I eat.'[22]

The two young women were noticed by a group of cavalry officers who came in for alterations, and they asked the girls if they would like to join them to watch a showjumping competition. The officers often invited the girls out for sherbets at popular tearoom La Tentation, to the art nouveau Grand Café, with huge gilded mirrors and plush seats, or to Les Palets d'Or chocolatier, featuring a blue swirling neoclassical facade, designed in 1898 by the Moulins School of Fine Arts.[23]

One of these officers was Étienne Balsan, completing his military training in Moulins with the Tenth Light Horse after spending time in Algeria. He was twenty-five years old, and cut a dashing figure with his tanned skin and moustache. His wealthy family, from Châteauroux, owned a thriving textile company that provided the blue cloth for British police uniforms. Étienne was sporty and restless, and having been educated at a British boarding school he relished polo, racing and fox-hunting. Horses were his first love, even above women. When his parents died, when he was eighteen, he inherited a fortune, but rather than follow his two brothers into the family textile business, he chose to spend his money on raising thoroughbred horses.[24]

There were expectations that Étienne should marry a respectable bourgeoisie, just as his brothers had, but he preferred the company of women from the *demimonde*, a class on the edge of respectability. Étienne was a nonconformist who flouted conventions, and spirited Gabrielle, a waif without parents or money, appealed to this nature. He adopted her into his circle of friends and affection and loyalty grew between them.

When younger sister Antoinette joined Gabrielle and Adrienne for dates with the cavalry officers, the women became known as the Three Graces. They were regularly invited to spend evenings with the officers at café-concert venue La Rotonde, an octagonal iron pavilion surrounded by gardens, which offered rowdy entertainments for the officers. Besides professional singers belting out tunes all evening, there were also the *poseuses* who sung between acts – girls with less experience who risked being pelted with cherry pits if they couldn't perform well enough.

Chanel was encouraged to get up and sing, and having a strong voice she was recruited by both La Rotonde and the Grand Café as a *poseuse*. Her repertoire included 'Qui qu'a vu' *Coco*, a popular ditty about a girl who loses her dog Coco at the Trocadéro amusement park in Paris. Another rendition was the 1897 smash hit 'Ko Ko Ri Ko', named after the French version of cock-a-doodle-do, the rooster's cry. Because of these songs, Étienne affectionately nicknamed Gabrielle La Petit Coco, and to further the joke, his friends nicknamed him Rico, to refer to them both as CocoRico.[25] Despite this legend of the name Coco being born amid the café concerts of Moulins, Gabrielle was adamant that it had been her father who had named her Coco. 'He used to call me Little Coco until something better should come along. He didn't like Gabrielle at all; it hadn't been his choice. And he was right...'[26]

Chanel was sometimes allowed to go to Vichy to visit her grandparents, and was taken with the magic of the fashionable spa resort, with its springs where the bourgeoisie flocked for restorative mineral waters. She adored the parks in which orchestras played in the bandstands, the cabaret acts in the Grand Casino, the elegant cafés and afternoon teas. 'Away from my chestnut groves, Vichy was a fairyland,' she told writer and friend Paul Morand. 'A ghastly fairyland in reality, but wonderful to fresh eyes.'[27]

Gabrielle believed she could find fame as a singer in the pleasure town, and she persuaded Adrienne to come with her. A photograph of the two women, taken in 1906, captures them in a Vichy park wearing homemade clothes: Gabrielle in a tailored jacket and skirt, with a frilled blouse to accentuate the severity of her suit. It's the earliest example of the Chanel style, which contrasted with the fashion at the time for restrictive, overly feminine clothing.

While longing to pick up work in concert halls as a *gommeuse*, a singer in a sequinned, cleavage-revealing gown, Gabrielle held a job as a dispenser in the pump room of the Grande Grille, dressed in a white uniform, like that of a nurse, serving mineral water from behind a grilled counter.[28]

Gabrielle auditioned for the Grand Casino, but her performance didn't impress, and she was ultimately disappointed that her dreams of being a singer, like those in the posters of Toulouse-Lautrec, had been dashed. When the 1907 season at Vichy was over, Chanel gave up and returned to Moulins, where Adrienne had fallen in love with Maurice, Baron de Gay de Nexon. His parents refused him permission to marry a girl of lowly standing, and so Adrienne could only be his mistress. Adrienne hoped she could find independence through love, while Gabrielle, or Coco as she was now known, was determined to find it through money and success.

Royallieu

When Étienne Balsan completed his military service at the end of 1904, he was free to devote himself to horse racing. He bought an estate, Royallieu, in the forest of Compiègne, northeast of Paris, a popular spot for racing and stag-hunting amongst the oak and beech trees.

Gabrielle (left) with Adrienne (right) in Vichy, 1906, in homemade clothes that showcase the early Chanel style.

The château was built on the site of a monastery in 1303, which had been converted to a defence post in the Middle Ages, a hunting lodge for kings and a convent for Benedictine nuns in the seventeenth century. The house, now covered in ivy, was Étienne's dream home, with paddocks for his horses, wild deer roaming in the meadows, and where he could entertain a stream of visitors, including his polo-playing circle of friends, actresses and courtesans.

Realising there wasn't much in Moulins for her, Coco followed Étienne to Royallieu, and by 1906 had moved into the château – her name appearing on the census returns along with a long list of jockeys, grooms and servants. She knew that she would struggle to marry well without a dowry, but perhaps Étienne could be a benefactor?[29]

On arrival, Coco soon discovered that Étienne's primary mistress was Émilienne d'Alençon, a renowned courtesan. Paris had an infamous system of prostitution in the belle époque era, and they inhabited the world of the *demimonde*. There were numerous names for courtesans – *cocotte*, *camélia*, after Alexandre Dumas's novel, *La Dame aux Camélias*, *les grandes horizontales*, and diamond crunchers, a category that Émilienne fell into for the way she could extract jewels from wealthy admirers.

Born in Paris, Émilienne began her career as a rabbit trainer in the circus, and was celebrated as a dancer in the Folies Bergère

The chateau at Royallieu, owned by Etienne Balsan before the First World War, and located in Parc de Bayser, Compiègne.

and as a star of ballets such as *La Belle et la Bête*. She was a frequent visitor to the theatres of Paris and the haunts of the *demimonde*, including Chez Maxim, where she enthralled Parisian high society. She earned a lofty reputation as one-time mistress of the King of Belgium, Leopold II, who bestowed her with pearls and precious stones and introduced her to the Prince of Wales and Kaiser Wilhelm II.

Émilienne was in her early thirties by the time Chanel met her, and while some may have thought she was over the hill, she still had the power to seduce. 'Étienne Balsan liked old women,' Chanel said bitterly on reflection to journalist and biographer Marcel Haedrich. She added that Étienne 'adored *cocottes* and he lived with that one to the scandal of his family'.[30] When Coco first arrived, there may have been times when she was left to eat her meals with the servants, while Étienne held dinners upstairs for society guests. But Étienne found Coco refreshing and amusing, and he liked having her around as a second mistress.

Paris was discovering the artists Henri Matisse and Pablo Picasso, but life at Royallieu revolved around horses. Chanel would watch the weigh-ins with the jockeys in their satin shirts at La Croix Saint Ouen, and would spend time in the stables with the grooms and fearlessly gallop on horseback through the Compiègne forest. She loved Longchamp, the racetrack at Bois de Boulogne, with the Eiffel Tower in the distance, the smell of fresh grass and the excitement of the finish line.

Royallieu was marked by idleness, with trips to the races and fancy-dress parties to break the boredom. In the mornings Chanel lounged on the terrace at Royallieu, scanning the racing results over breakfast and coffee. In one photograph, she is a pre-Raphaelite heroine with a blanket on her lap and her long, dark hair falling loose onto her shoulders as she reads a newspaper. Étienne recalled how 'she would lie in bed until noon, drinking coffee and milk and reading cheap novels'.[31]

Regular visitors to Royallieu were the actress Gabrielle Dorziat, lover of Count Léon de Laborde; Marthe Davelli, a young opera singer; and beautiful Suzanne Orlandi, Baron Henri de Foy's mistress. Chanel was fascinated with the *cocottes*, much more so than the society women, or 'proper' ladies whom she sometimes encountered. 'I was very hard on all those ladies, especially the society women, whom I considered dirty,' she said. 'But I thought the *cocottes* were ravishing, with their hats that were too big and their heavy make-up. They were so appetising! They resembled my novels. The kept women and the world they lived in were my stories.'[32]

She spoke of the clothes the women wore at the races, with their 'enormous loaves on their heads, constructions made of feathers and improved with fruits and plumes; but worst of all, which appalled me, their hats did not fit on their heads'.[33] It was easier to make fun of them than to try and be part of the social hierarchy, and so she deliberately chose to be different. She was comparable to the character of 'Claudine' in Colette's popular series of belle époque novels – a motherless convent schoolgirl who becomes involved in Paris's avant-garde circles. Coco dressed 'like a schoolgirl. I couldn't dress any other way. At eighteen I looked fifteen.'[34]

As well as ordering a tailored tweed jacket to be custom-made for her, Coco borrowed items from male wardrobes, such as a shirt with knitted tie and simple hat, or jodhpurs from a groom, so she could straddle the horse rather than go side saddle. A photograph from 1907 captures Coco and Adrienne at the races, with Coco in a simple straw hat and gown with a little white collar, which she had made herself. Another photograph depicts her standing on a bench at the racecourse at Midi, wearing her own straw boater with huge hatpin and in a heavy overcoat borrowed from Baron Foy and a shirt and tie from Étienne, which she had snipped to alter. Étienne was annoyed that she had cut his best shirt, but Coco was forceful enough to get away with it.

Coco had, on one of her few trips to Paris, visited Galeries Lafayette, where she bought basic straw boaters and decorated them simply with ribbons and hatpins. She wore her straw boater hats 'perfectly straight – in those days they were usually tilted and covered with birds' nests. Everyone admired them, so I thought: why not actually make them?' She created one for Émilienne to wear to the races, and immediately other women were curious to know where she got such a novel hat.[35]

When Coco turned twenty-five, in 1908, she wondered about her future – she didn't want to be reliant on other people,

instead she needed to find an occupation. One morning on the terrace, she mentioned to Étienne how popular her hats were with the ladies. At first he was dismissive, but when she pressed him again, he eventually agreed to help her. He offered up his Parisian bachelor apartment as a base for selling her hats. Besides, he was planning to go to Argentina, racehorse capital of the Americas, and was keen to give her something to do in his absence.

But beforehand, Étienne made his annual autumn trip to Pau, in the Pyrenees, where he would stay in a thirteenth-century château and fox-hunt and play polo. He invited her to come along. Gabrielle loved the quiet of the place, the 'green pastures, the mountain streams rushing to the plains, the grass-covered jumps and the hunters in their red coats'. It was also where she would lay her eyes on Arthur 'Boy' Capel for the first time.[36]

Coco in the grandstands in 1907 with Adrienne, wearing a simple straw hat and gown with a white collar, which she made herself.

2 Genre Pauvre

'The young man was handsome, very tanned and attractive. More than handsome, he was magnificent...He rode bold and very powerful horses. I fell in love with him.'

Paris, Deauville, Biarritz
1908–1919

'Does the name "Boy" Capel mean anything to you?', Chanel asked English journalist Malcolm Muggeridge in September 1944, when he interviewed her at her rue Cambon salon just after the liberation of Paris. 'He was the man I loved. A true dandy.'[37] It had been Boy who had helped her find the freedom to navigate her way from Royallieu to bustling belle époque Paris.

Coco Chanel met Arthur 'Boy' Capel forty years earlier, in 1908, while in Pau with Étienne. 'We made each other's acquaintance when we were out horse trekking one day; we all lived on horseback,' she told Paul Morand. 'The young man was handsome, very tanned and attractive. More than handsome, he was magnificent. I admired his nonchalance, and his green eyes. He rode bold and very powerful horses. I fell in love with him. I had never loved.'[38]

With her keen sense of smell, she was attracted by his fragrance of leather, vegetation, horses and saddle soap. She remembered a day they spent riding together in the rain, and in the evening warming by the fire in the manor hall, sipping cognac with Étienne. She remembered that Boy left Pau to take the sleeper train to Paris, she followed after him, and he scooped her up and carried her into his berth.[39] Whether this account is fanciful is unclear, but back at Royallieu, Boy was swept away with Chanel's charm. He admired her spark, her sharp tongue, her wit and energy, and he liked adventurous women. He was dashing and charming and, like Chanel, had good taste and elegance.

Arthur Capel was born in Brighton, England, in September 1881, to a wealthy Catholic family, rich from coal mining. With a French mother and English father, Boy was bilingual and spent part of his childhood in Paris. He was sent to the Catholic boarding school Beaumont College, followed by Downside, in England, where he excelled at polo. His was a life of privilege, and close friends included Duc Armand de Gramont, Comte de Guiche and the English aristocratic polo set. Chanel later said of Boy that he 'was one of the lions of London society' and 'he is the

Arthur 'Boy' Capel in 1911 at his 138 boulevard Malesherbes apartment. He was a wealthy business owner, playboy and voracious reader.

man I have loved. He is dead. I have never forgotten him. He was the great stroke of luck in my life.'[40]

Gabrielle arrived in Paris with just a few belongings, including an alpaca suit and a goatskin jacket, and opened her hat shop in Étienne's ground-floor apartment at 160 boulevard Malesherbes. Capel helped with a bank account for her and, quite unconventionally, she moved into an apartment with him on avenue Gabriel. Étienne taught Coco to ride, while Boy, a keen motorist, taught her to drive; both were in love with her.

'It was a lucky thing for me that I had read all those books, because I came to Paris at a very romantic time, the time of the Ballets Russes,' Coco said. Paris was pulsing with excitement, and was a city of art nouveau posters and architecture, where the leading designer was Paul Poiret. His freedom-giving designs included the corset-free kimono coat and harem pants, shaped by the fashion for Orientalism, also seen in Sergei Diaghilev's

Left: Chanel shared an apartment with Boy Capel on quiet, tree-lined avenue Gabriel, by the Jardin des Champs-Élysées.

Right: The Alphonse Mucha art nouveau poster for the 1896 production of La Dame aux Camélias, starring Sarah Bernhardt, which enchanted young Gabrielle.

Ballets Russes. The exotic, ornate costumes and set designs, and the hypnotising movements of dancer Vaslav Nijinsky, amazed the audience, transporting them to fantastical worlds.

Chanel recalled she had visited Paris with Adrienne on one occasion to see Sarah Bernhardt in *La Dame aux Camélias*. Bernhardt famously played her as an art nouveau heroine on stage at the Renaissance theatre in 1896, when Coco was thirteen. The tragic romance stirred within her a memory of her mother and a bloody handkerchief, and inspired a future love of camellias. '*La Dame aux Camélias* was my life, all the trashy novels I'd fed on,' she said. She also remembered on that visit that 'we got in at the Gare de Lyon and stayed at the Terminus Hotel at the Gare Saint-Lazare. The heat! I hated it. I could hardly walk on the thick nailed-down carpets – I was used to polished floors.'[41]

Chanel thrived in the city but the world of high society was overwhelming. The Parisian *gratin,* or upper crust, were anglophiles who loved sport and riding in motorcars, and Boy and Étienne were part of this group. 'When I came to Paris, I had to learn everything,' she told Marcel Haedrich. 'I'd never before ridden in a vehicle with pneumatic tyres – I'd ridden in cars with solid tyres. They were so ugly! And the poor coachman who had to drive them, sitting out front and so high up.'[42] Visiting the Hôtel Ritz, she saw a lift for the first time in her life, and was unsure whether she should make conversation with the other passengers.[43]

The Paris Exposition of 1878 unveiled ambitious constructions in the city, including the formidable Eiffel Tower, while the Exposition of 1900 launched the Métropolitain underground system, which offered new freedoms for women now able to travel by themselves. By 1905 the first motorbuses appeared on the streets, yet women still navigated transport in long skirts, heels and precarious hats.

Paris was also home to *le grand magasin*, the department store, an Aladdin's cave set in ornate, imposing buildings on impressive boulevards, and it was at Galeries Lafayette that Chanel bought the cheap straw boaters to make her hats, adding 'just a touch of something on top'.[44]

Chanel's first clients at boulevard Malesherbes were Étienne's former mistresses and companions, and word of Coco's simple hats soon spread. They were the antithesis of the fashionable

confections normally worn. Her first piece of publicity came in September 1910, when actress Lucienne Roger, wearing a Chanel-designed 'bird of paradise hat', appeared on the front cover of the magazine *Comoedia Illustré*.[45] Chanel's hats were so well received that, in the October 1910 issue of the magazine, she modelled one of her wide, plumed hats herself.[46] Gabrielle Dorziat, one of Paris's leading actresses and an acquaintance from Royallieu, was heralded by the press for her style, and she was photographed wearing Chanel's hats in Paris fashion magazines, as well as on stage in Guy de Maupassant's *Bel Ami*, in which she wore a tricorn velvet hat.[47] Actress Suzanne Orlandi was photographed sporting a Chanel hat and a long, black, velvet dress with white collar, made from instructions by Chanel, and possibly the first example of a dress in her style that she sold.[48]

Arthur Capel assisted with funds to lease a mezzanine at 21 rue Cambon, which opened in January 1910, with 'Chanel Modes' printed proudly above the door. This little street was in the heart of the fashion district of the 1st arrondissement, where major designers, milliners and jewellers owned boutiques. Other up-and-coming female designers included Madeleine Vionnet, who opened her boutique on rue de Rivoli in 1912, and Jeanne Lanvin, who set up her own loft in 22 rue du Faubourg Saint-Honoré. Another advantage of rue Cambon was that it had an entrance to the Ritz. It was also populated by the renowned restaurant Voisin's, and Smith's English tearoom, a particular favourite for belle époque ladies seeking respite while shopping.[49]

Chanel's shop was becoming such a success that she hired Adrienne and Antoinette as sales assistants and to promote the Chanel Modes brand. The period between 1910 and 1914 was one of the happiest times of her life, when her business was taking off and she was in love with Boy in Paris. Boy was connected to artists, writers, politicians and sportsmen, and Chanel was soon mixing in these circles. Her relationship with Boy also made her a curiosity among the ladies, whom she charged as much as she could get away with.

Coco demonstrated her early interior design skills on the 'delightful' apartment on avenue Gabriel that she shared with Boy. When looking for pieces to furnish the place, she saw a Coromandel screen for the first time, and was struck by its beauty, recalling that she thought 'I'd faint with joy'.[50]

These Chinese wood-lacquered screens took their name from their shipping route from China to Europe via Madras, on the Coromandel Coast. 'There's something compelling and irrevocable about it that appealed to me,' she said. 'Screens were the first thing I ever bought. You don't come across them much in the provinces, of course. I'd never seen anything like it. The people I knew were more likely to buy a store-cupboard for sheets dried in the sun.' She loved the glossy black lacquer with gold, silver and red birds, flowers and pavilions. That they could

be folded up and taken anywhere appealed to her, too. 'They play the role that tapestries did in the Middle Ages; they allow you to recreate your home everywhere,' she said.[51]

Her interior choice for the apartment represented an early version of her favourite colours and style. She dyed the rugs beige as the colour 'reminded me of the soil', and the theme was carried through with natural, unpainted wood and beige furnishings. She chose so much beige that 'the day came when the interior designers begged for mercy', and persuaded her to try draping white satin. She chose English silverware, 'expensively designed rice papers', and tall vases filled with white flowers were artfully placed in the rooms.[52]

French playwright Henri Bernstein often came for dinner with his wife Antoinette, and they both remarked on how beautiful the apartment was. Chanel spent many happy days there with Boy, staying in rather than going out. 'I dressed in the evening to please Capel, knowing very well that there would shortly be a

Gabrielle Chanel in 1910, wearing a dazzling white satin gown, the favoured fabric for draping in her avenue Gabriel apartment.

moment when he would say: "why go out, after all, we're very comfortable here". He liked me among my surroundings, and there's a girl-from-the-harem side of me which suited this seclusion very well.'[53]

When she was able to go for evenings out with Boy, 'she was envied because she had tamed the lion of the city's nights'.[54] They sometimes went to Chez Maxim or to the Café de Paris, where she wore a clinging blue and white grosgrain gown from a Parisian couturier. She recalled it was so tight she had to ask Boy to undo it for her, but after having eaten, and with a full stomach, she couldn't do it up again. Not having a coat to hide her shame, she promised herself she wouldn't ever wear another corset. [55]

Chanel was aware that Boy was seeing other women, but she chose to ignore the fact and follow the nonconformist attitude of Balsan's circle at Royallieu. On one occasion at the Deauville Casino, when she was dressed in a dazzlingly simple white dress, she felt all eyes were on the glamour couple, as the women lusted after Boy and were curious about her. 'All the women ran after him. I wasn't jealous.'[56]

After seeing Isadora Duncan dance at the Gaîté Lyrique, Gabrielle was inspired to take lessons from Elise Toulemon, also known as Caryathis, and she would climb up to the Butte every morning to reach Toulemon's studio on rue Lamarck in Montmartre. Despite the lessons, she was told she had limited talent to go further, but it was Caryathis, one of the first women in Paris to cut her hair, who invited her to the infamous opening night of Stravinsky's *The Rite of Spring* at the new Theatre des Champs Élysées on 13 May 1913.[57] The ballet, with its primitive choreography to Stravinsky's pulsating, jarring composition, was so daring that the audience were shocked into rioting. Chanel would also climb up the steps to Picasso's Montmartre studio at Bateau-Lavoir, 13 rue Ravignan, which she called an 'alchemist's den'.

Deauville

Boy Capel took Chanel to Deauville in the summer of 1913, where he booked a prime suite at the newly opened Hôtel Normandy. With its charming streets of neo-Norman buildings, chalk cliffs flanking a long sweep of golden sand and the bracing waters of the English Channel, Deauville was the French summer resort for the wealthy and connected at the turn of the twentieth century. *Vogue* magazine named it 'the summer capital of France', with the 'shortest, gayest and most exciting season of any of the fashionable resorts on the continent'. The season was centred around the horse races at Deauville racetrack, built in 1862 by the Duke of Morny. Activities included yachting, boating, racing, polo and gambling at the Deauville Casino, where one went to see and to be seen.

In September 1913, the *New York Times* announced: 'One of the most fashionable spots in Europe during August is Deauville, down on the coast. Here we all troop like countrymen to a circus. And we see sights, too. Gowns that are unbelievable, jewels that must have been found by Sinbad the Sailor, hats that could never be worn by Americans, bathing suits that would shock even Atlantic City – here they all are, gathered together under one blue sky.'[58]

The article recounted how the schedule in Deauville was to bathe at 11a.m., then parade along smart rue Gontaut Biron and enjoy an *apéritif* and *déjeuner* at the Hôtel Royale or the Normandy, attend the races in the afternoon, eat dinner at 9p.m. and then visit the Casino after 11p.m.[59]

With magazines lauding the summer fashion parades at the beach resort, Boy encouraged Gabrielle to open a new boutique on rue Gontaut Biron – an ideal location close to the Normandy, the casino and the beach. The name 'Gabrielle Chanel' was boldly printed in black on a white awning, and curious ladies were soon flocking to the boutique, which sold a revolutionary line in beachwear. The fashion in summer 1913 was for Paul Poiret-style tunics in the evenings, but soon Chanel's name was

The beach huts at Deauville, with its fairy-tale neo-Norman townhouses behind.

also on the list of what to wear. She was even given a name-check in the *New York Times* that year, for her morning coats.[60]

In those days, women covered up completely on the beach, in order to protect their skin from the sun. But Chanel had a fresh take on time spent at a beach resort, creating clothes that were cooler and less restrictive. Chanel's fashion line included turtlenecks, linen skirts, sailor's blouses and belted jersey sweaters based on Boy's polo shirts, which she had borrowed on occasion, rolling up the sleeves and tying a handkerchief around the waist.

Another influence was her nephew's English school uniform of navy-blue sweaters and blazers. When her older sister Julie-Berthe died suddenly, she left behind a six-year-old boy, André, and with Boy's help Coco agreed to take responsibility and sent

Chanel modelling her Deauville collection on the Étretat beach in Normandy, with the chalk cliffs of Falaise D'Amont in the background.

him to Beaumont, Boy's old school in England.[61] Chanel also admired the Normandy fishermen she saw in Deauville, inspiring a taste for striped tops. *Women's Wear Daily* reported on Deauville and Chanel in summer 1915, praising her striped sweaters, which could be slipped on over the head. They were made from jersey, which at the time was considered a 'poor' fabric. 'A great success is predicted for these sweaters.'[62]

Chanel's relaxed silhouette broke from the restrictive corseted fashions, allowing women to gain their independence. Sports clothes were slowly inching into women's wardrobes with the invention of the bicycle and the introduction of motorcars, for which goggles, duster coats and veils were essential.

Chanel created 'long and ample coats with great pockets', where the workman-style pockets were designed to free women from their handbags and to help navigate Paris's modern transport. Chanel also liberated the ankle, making it easier to climb into motorcars without having to lift the skirt daintily.

With her defiant sense of style, Chanel was the perfect model for her own clothes, and she was photographed in 1913 next to colourful Normandy beach huts, her hands thrust into her pockets, wearing a loose-belted coat and pale ankle-length skirt. She was also photographed outside her shop, posing again with her hands in the pockets of a belted tunic, narrow white skirt and a blouse with sailor collar.

'Everybody wanted to meet me,' she recalled of the time. 'I became something of a celebrity, and there, too, I started a fashion – couturières as stars. Before my time that didn't exist.' Among the more high-profile guests to her boutique were Baroness Diane 'Kitty' de Rothschild and Parisian actress Cécile Sorel. Antoinette Bernstein, wife of Henri, said in the 1970s: 'I'm not quite sure when I met Coco Chanel for the first time, but she was a young woman, not yet thirty, and physically absolutely charming. It was the time of Deauville's revival, and I loved to see what was in her boutique. Then, in Paris, I went again.'[63]

Such was Coco's new fame, that she was depicted in Deauville by cartoonist Sem in *Le Figaro*, running into the arms of Boy as a polo-playing centaur. Paul Morand, her lifelong friend, was also inspired to write his novel *Lewis et Irène*, based on the love story of Boy and Coco.

It was the height of the Deauville season, during a heatwave in August 1914, when war in Europe broke out. Luxury boutiques closed down overnight, the price of petrol rocketed and the season's regulars abandoned the resort. Boy Capel persuaded Chanel to stay in Deauville rather than flee to Paris, as he was also renting a villa at which to keep his ponies while he went to the front. By the end of August, when the Germans marched closer to Paris, wealthy women returned to Deauville for safety.

'One world was ending, another was about to be born. I was in the right place; an opportunity beckoned, I took it,' Chanel reflected. The carefree endless-summer life of the belle époque was over, and as men went to fight on the front, women's roles in society shifted dramatically and adapted to war. Cotton overalls, heavy overcoats, trenchcoats and shorter hemlines all served to help women carry out their new wartime roles in factories and as ambulance drivers. Luxury was considered inappropriate, and instead of the pre-war froufrou, the impression was to do one's bit. Chanel was quick to take advantage of the mood, and as the only boutique open in Deauville, customers came to her for the comfortable, loose clothing of her long jackets, linen skirts and sailor's blouses.

She told Paul Morand of the great success she experienced as a result of her practical designs. 'Many elegant ladies had come to Deauville. Not only did they need to have hats made for them, but soon, because there were no dressmakers, they had to be properly attired. I only had milliners with me: I converted them into dressmakers. There was a shortage of material. I cut jersey from the sweaters the stable lads wore and from the knitted training garments that I wore myself. By the end of the first summer of the war, I had earned two hundred thousand gold francs.'[64]

Gabrielle returned to Paris at the end of the year, as she wanted to be closer to Boy. Despite the war, Paris society tried to continue as normal. Chanel Modes was in a perfect position near the Ritz, as the hotel was a popular place for ladies to meet allied officers who, as Elizabeth de Gramont commented, could 'rub shoulders in the best heated interior in Paris'.[65]

With coal a precious commodity, women wore more animal skins and furs to keep warm. 'If there is no coal in the grate the

'One world was ending, another was about to be born. I was in the right place; an opportunity beckoned, I took it.'

It was in the Belle Époque beach resort of Deauville that Chanel made her name with a revolutionary line in beach clothing.

Parisienne wraps her fur coat about her, sets a remarkable hat upon her head, and sallies forth chic and warm,' noted British *Vogue* in September 1917.[66] But many of the popular skins were hard to come by, and Chanel began using rabbit fur – considered a peasant item – for her upmarket clothes. 'I had decided to replace expensive furs with the humblest hides. Chinchilla no longer arrived from South America, or sable from the Russia of the tsars. I used rabbit. In this way, I made poor people and small retailers wealthy; the large stores have never forgiven me.'[67]

Boy was given leave in the summer of 1915, and he took Coco to Biarritz. It was here that he encouraged her to open another shop in order to replicate Deauville's success, and she rented a space in the Villa de Larralde on rue Gardères, a romantic-looking faux-château with turrets. Opened on 15 July 1915, it was Biarritz's first fashion house, and Antoinette arrived from Paris to manage it, along with seamstresses from rue Cambon.

Close to the Spanish border, the ritzy Atlantic coast retreat was particularly popular with the Spanish aristocracy, who were untouched by the war. The Miramar and Hôtel du Palais were the chic spots for dancing all night, and Coco and Boy were invited for an evening out with Constant Say and opera singer Marthe Davelli, who lived on the Basque coast near Saint-Jean-de-Luz. Chanel and Boy also played golf and sunbathed on the beach with Pierre Decourcelle, the writer of Coco's beloved childhood romance novels. On the beach, Gabrielle and Marthe were doing something completely new and controversial for women – allowing their skin to tan.[68]

It was fabric manufacturer Jean Rodier who provided Chanel with a large stock of jersey to further develop her designs in this 'poor' fabric. In 1916 Rodier had a quantity of machine-knit jersey he couldn't use, as it was too scratchy for sports underwear, and so Chanel offered to buy it from him at a discount. The jersey was a natural cream colour, and she went on to collaborate with Rodier to develop jersey in grey, navy blue and coral for her frocks.[69]

Harper's Bazaar, in 1916, featured the first illustration of a Chanel gown. Part of the Biarritz collection, it was a V-neck

Coco Chanel playing golf around 1910, wearing her version of loose, practical sportswear.

chemise dress with embroidery and a low sash, fastened at the front.[70] In July of that same year British *Vogue* reported that 'Paris can think of nothing but jersey these days. (Chanel) took quantities of it, Bordeaux red in colour, and with the assistance of brown rabbit, somehow evolved a wrap which was a trio of capes, heaped one upon the other.'[71]

In August 1916, the fashion periodical continued: 'Paris can think of but two things – war and jersey; for jersey is no longer a fabric, it is an obsession.' The magazine would point out that 'Wool jersey cloth is practical, economical and smart, three very desirable qualities for the wartime purchaser.'[72]

With her rabbit fur and jersey fabrics, Chanel was leading the way in utilising poor fabrics, but selling them for upmarket prices. As Janet Flanner wrote in the *New Yorker* in 1931: 'Gabrielle Chanel is a dressmaker who grew rich launching the *genre pauvre*.'

'When I went to the races, I would never have thought that I was witnessing the death of luxury, the passing of the nineteenth century, the end of an era,' Chanel said. 'An age of magnificence, but of decadence, the last reflections of a baroque style in which the ornate had killed off the figure, in which over-embellishment had stifled the body's architecture, just as parasites smother trees in tropical forests.'[73]

One of Chanel's seamstresses, Marie-Louise Deray, recalled the demands of working with jersey, and with Chanel. 'The "diagonals" went every which way and we had to start over again several times. Mademoiselle was demanding. If a fitting went wrong she exploded. She loved to pester people. I cried a lot, believe me. She was tough, unrelenting with the staff. But what she came up with was sensational, both chic and exceedingly simple, so different from Poiret and Madeleine Vionnet.'

Most of Chanel's customers in Biarritz were Spanish, including Madrid royalty – Don Alfonso XIII, Princess Victoria Eugenie of Battenberg – who wanted colourful clothing that reflected the country's neutrality during the war. Deray described the workroom as 'an enchantment of colours, a rainbow', and that 'We did lovely things. In jersey, of course, but also in cotton. The straight tunic, with a large tied bow low over the hips, became fashionable.'[74]

From winter 1916, the *chemise* was the new silhouette. British *Vogue* said: 'Chanel still ties her narrow belts carelessly in front,

Chanel's jersey suits with loose belted jackets were much sought after during the First World War, as illustrated in magazine *Les Elegances Parisiennes* in March 1917.

but she, like the others, also uses the sectional belt, placed rather low.' Following Chanel's lead, Lanvin, Worth and Paquin created their own *chemises*.

It wasn't just simple navy, beige and grey jersey Chanel specialised in – she was creating crepe de Chine day dresses in dark blue, red and black, with Eastern-inspired embroidery. A black dress in November 1916 contrasted white embroidery of irises or Japanese cherry blossoms, tapping into the trend for 'brilliant Byzantine thread and Japanese embroidery'.[75] Chanel's gowns were quite different from the fashion for heavy taffeta, as they were light, and elegant, shimmering with metallic lace and beading.

In spring 1918, the Germans shelled Paris from a long-range gun, and during one heavy night of bombing, guests at the Ritz were guided to the basement to take safety. The next day ladies went to Chanel's to find nightwear suitable for wearing in bomb shelters, and Chanel improvised with a set of red men's pyjamas, which were quickly snapped up. She then produced pyjamas in pale silk, and these again proved very popular, despite it being very daring for a woman to wear trousers in public.

Chanel's style was a new fashion for a new era, and it heralded a slimmer look for women. 'Since they ate a great deal, they were stout, and since they were stout and didn't want to be, they strapped themselves in,' she said of women before the war. 'By inventing the jersey, I liberated the body, I discarded the waist (and only reverted to it in 1930), I created a new shape; in order to conform to it all my customers, with the help of the war, became slim, "slim like Coco".'[76]

Even after peace was declared, the legacy of wartime clothing remained. Skirt lengths sat just above the ankles, and tailored jackets flared at the hip, so women could more easily enjoy walking as a hobby or taking part in sports. British *Vogue*, in autumn 1919, noted: 'We know very well that sports and open-air living are the best of all ways of preserving our youth and the suppleness of our figures.'[77]

Before the war, women weren't allowed into the bar at the Ritz unchaperoned, but postwar Paris had many new possibilities and freedoms. Chanel's clothes fulfilled a range of activities; sportswear for tennis and golf, and gowns for the casino or the races, offering the allusion of austerity, but with a price tag for the wealthy. 'A dress made right should allow one to walk, to dance, even to ride horseback!' she said.[78]

Three Chanel outfits were featured in British *Vogue* on the re-opening of the races at Longchamp and Auteuil. There was a grey and black satin cape for wrapping up in a motorcar, a black satin coat with fringing, inspired by American cowboys, and the first example of Chanel's little black dress – a thin black lace dress over a hoop, with pleated black pantaloons underneath and a ribbon at the waist.[79]

Boy Capel had become even richer from coal during the war, and he also found literary success with *Reflections on Victory*, a book calling for a peaceful solution to war. He had a deep sense of the theosophical, of signs and symbols and religious theories, which heavily influenced Chanel's life. But he also needed to marry well, and he broke the news to Gabrielle that he was engaged to be married to Lady Diana Wyndham, a

'By inventing the jersey, I liberated the body, I discarded the waist. I created a new shape; in order to conform to it all my customers, with the help of the war, became slim, "slim like Coco".'

war widow who had worked as an ambulance driver for the Red Cross. Boy hoped that Chanel would remain in his life as his mistress, but she moved out of the apartment in avenue Gabriel that she had so thoughtfully decorated. She often stayed in a quiet villa, La Milanaise, in the Paris suburb of Rueil, which she acquired to mark the end of the war and which offered lovely views of the city. Boy continued to visit her frequently despite now being married, often complaining to her how unhappy he was with Diana.[80]

Just before Christmas 1919 he visited Coco in his fashionable new car, before driving overnight to the Riviera with plans to spend the festive season with his sister and his wife. But he never made it there, as he died in a horrific car accident not far from Nice, in the early hours of 22 December.

The Times of London reported on 24 December 1919 that 'Captain Capel had been killed owing to one of the tyres of his car bursting, and that his chauffeur, named Mansfield, had been injured.' *The Times* also reported that 'Captain Capel's death is a great blow to his many friends in Paris. He was probably one of the best-known Englishmen living in France, where he had important coal interests. During the war he did excellent liaison work … he was a thorough sportsman, and at the same time a lover of books.'[81]

It was Comte Léon de Laborde, a friend from Royallieu, who broke the news to Chanel before dawn on 22 December. He continuously rang the doorbell of her Ruiel home before Joseph, her butler, answered the door and reluctantly agreed to wake her. She stood at the top of the stairs, in white pyjamas, her short hair messed from sleep, looking to him like 'the silhouette of a youth in white satin'. She quietly packed an overnight bag, and she and Comte Léon drove south to Monte Carlo, where Boy's sister was staying.[82]

After resting on a chaise longue in Capel's sister's suite, Chanel asked to be taken to the scene of the crash. The burned-out car was off the road, and she sat by it on the kilometre stone, crying for the loss. It was a final, devastating blow after his marriage. 'In losing Capel, I lost everything.'[83]

Carl Erickson

E. Chanel
"403"
Credit: Wanamaker

D. Chanel
"489"
Credit: Wanamaker

150

3 Bohemian Paris

Paris
1919–1929

If there was one time and place that defined Coco Chanel, it was Paris in the 1920s, that exciting, frivolous era, known in France as *les années folles*. After the First World War, the city became a mecca for the beautiful and the talented looking to forget the horrors they had experienced. Coco was the fashion vanguard of the era, capturing the mood of the time and shaping the way women dressed. 'I was working towards a new society,' Coco said. 'Up until then they had been clothes designed for women who were useless and idle, women whose lady's maids had to pass them their stockings; I now had customers who were busy women; a busy woman needs to feel comfortable in her clothes. You need to be able to roll up your sleeves.'[1]

It was Chanel's style that defined the look of '*la garçonne*', also known as the 'flapper'. These were modern women who were energetic and amorous, who cut their hair short and raised their hems, who drank champagne and cocktails, smoked cigarettes and wore rouge. Forward-thinking fashion illustrations began depicting women applying lipstick or smoking, reinforcing this emancipated way of living. Chanel's flirtations, her friends and her lovers were a roll call of the leading artists and writers of that generation – Pablo Picasso, Christian Bérard, Serge Lifar, Jean Cocteau, Igor Stravinsky and poets Raymond Radiguet and Pierre Reverdy. Chanel said that only in Paris would these meetings have been possible, where artists, aristocrats and Russian refugees collided. 'People don't live in the Auvergne, and you don't spend your life in Málaga, or in Barcelona.'[2]

While cubism had been born in Montmartre, the district was considered passé in the postwar years, now the haunt of opium smokers and prostitutes. The real artists and bohemians had moved to Montparnasse on the Left Bank, dressing like the Americans who were spending carelessly. Ernest Hemingway was one of the Lost Generation – those who were drawn to Paris to escape the scars of war, and who lived as nihilists and hedonists. The city was alive with all-night cocktail parties and fancy-dress balls, inspired by the masquerade carnivals of seventeenth-century Venice.

Illustration by Carl Erickson for *Vogue*, 1927, featuring two Chanel gowns. On the left is 403, a black mousseline evening dress, and on the right is 489, a black satin gown.

PROGRAMME OFFICIEL DES BALLETS RUSSES

Costume de "NARCISSE"

'After my days spent working in the rue Cambon, interrupted by a hurried tea at Fleurs, in the Faubourg Saint-Honoré, I didn't much feel like going out,' Coco confessed. 'Yet Paris, at that time, was experiencing its strangest and most brilliant years. London and New York (I'm not talking about Berlin, which was buckling then under the throes of devaluation, hunger and expressionism) had their eyes trained on us. From the rue Cambon to Montparnasse, I watched as the Faubourg Saint-Germain attuned itself, princesses opened tea shops that bore the names of well-known books, the White Russians landed, and Europe patched things up for one last time as best it could.'[3]

Gabrielle loved ballet, and found the exotic spectacle of the Ballets Russes particularly intoxicating. 'You can't imagine how beautiful they are,' she said. 'Once you've seen them your life will be completely different.'[4] In the 1910s, the Ballets Russes had helped shape a love for exotic and Oriental designs in Paris, and following the revolution of 1917, Russian designers, evoking their folk traditions and arts, swept Paris with their heritage. Sylvia Lyon once wrote in her column: 'Sergei Diaghilev used to say that the Ballets Russes would be a success if, on opening night, Coco Chanel and Jean Cocteau were in the audience.'

The war was still raging when Gabrielle met the woman who would be both a thorn and a rose in her life, Misia Sert, who introduced her to the most influential, artistic people in Paris. In May 1917, the Parisian avant-garde sought much-needed escapism in *Parade*, a cubist ballet by Jean Cocteau, with sets and costumes designed by Pablo Picasso. The premiere took place on 18 May 1917, at the Théâtre du Châtelet, and Chanel arrived on the arm of Boy Capel in her red velvet, fur-trimmed coat, sporting a new bobbed haircut that was the talk of the evening amongst this creative circle. She told a story that her long hair had been burned when her gas boiler blew up at avenue Gabriel, just before she was due to go to the opera, so she took the scissors and cut off her hair. She told Paul Morand: 'Everyone went into raptures, saying that I looked like "a young boy, a little shepherd".'[5] The writer Colette had shorn her hair in 1903, similarly justifying the act by saying she had burnt it on an oil lamp – short hair on women was considered so scandalous that it could only be accidental.

The evening of the premiere, actress Cécile Sorel, also showing off a new short haircut, held a dinner at her chic apartment with its leopardskin drapes, and invited Arthur and Gabrielle – the bachelor and his artist girlfriend.

Coco was a fascinating creature in the eyes of one of Paris's most influential women, Misia Sert. Misia, born Maria Godebska in St Petersburg, in 1872, was the high priestess of the art world. She had been painted by Pierre Auguste Renoir, Henri Toulouse-Lautrec and Édouard Vuillard, and was muse to Marcel Proust, Claude Debussy and Maurice Ravel. She had married newspaper magnate Alfred Edwards, but was now with painter José-Maria Sert, who created huge frescos and murals for the ballroom of the Waldorf-Astoria hotel in New York, and subsequently for the Rockefeller Center. As Paul Morand said, she was a collector of geniuses, all of whom seemed to fall in love with her.

'In my case, I sometimes bite my friends, but Misia, she devours them,' Coco once said. She added that 'Misia has the most serious virtue of all: she's never boring, even though she's always bored. To distract her – everything to do with me amused her – and to inflame her curiosity, I invented bogus love affairs, imaginary passions. She was always taken in.'[6]

On that evening in 1917, Chanel described Misia as having a 'little chignon in the shape of a shell, with a sort of mandarin orange stuck on the top of her head'. Misia, who had been in awe of Chanel's red velvet coat and asked to borrow it, grabbed the designer after dinner, and insisted she visit her apartment overlooking the Seine, on the corner of the rue de Beaune. In her salon, Misia regularly served lobster on silver platters, and kept a blue macaw to entertain guests, but Coco wasn't impressed with the clutter she found in the home – collections of fans, ornaments and gatherings of dust.

'When I saw all that pile of objects, I thought she must be an antique dealer. Capel, who came with me, thought so too. He asked, quite shamelessly: "Is it for sale?" Those fish in aquariums, those ships in bottles … I was appalled. It smelt of filth downstairs; there was no surface upon which you could use a duster or apply any polish; scarcely a flurry from that horrible object … all she likes is mother-of-pearl; a nostalgia for vases probably. Luxury for her is the opposite of luxury. For Misia, it's the flea market.'[7]

Misia would become Chanel's closest female friend and helped ingratiate her into bohemian Paris. The central gathering place for the city's avant-garde was Le Boeuf sur le Toit, on rue Boissy d'Anglas, which opened in 1921, and where Gabrielle could be found at least once a week with great artists and musicians. Also known as The Nothing Doing Bar, it was bustling and chaotic, and a place for cross-dressing, for opium, morphine and cocaine, beloved by Jean Cocteau, the lesbian Princess Violette Murat, and Les Six, the group of young Montparnasse composers. Diaghilev's premiere party for Stravinsky's ballet *Les noces* was held at Le Boeuf sur le Toit in June 1923, while American socialites Sara and Gerald Murphy hosted an infamous party there, also for Stravinsky.

Count Étienne de Beaumont's spring costume parties were the highlight of Paris society. The Beaumont's salon was on rue Masseran, where they frequently held Les Soirées de Paris, a spectacle of dance and pantomime, and it sought always to avoid being 'old hat'.[8]

Misia Sert, Chanel's closest female friend, in a portrait taken in the early 1920s.

For 1919, the theme was to 'leave exposed that part of one's body one finds the most interesting'. Chanel was asked to design some of the costumes, but when Misia enquired with the Count as to whether Chanel would also be invited to the ball, de Beaumont dismissed her – Chanel was considered a seamstress, and he would never invite *tradespeople*. In protest, Misia, Sert and Picasso refused to attend his ball, but in only a couple of years the tables would turn as Chanel's stature grew, her fame reached beyond societal conventions, and it was de Beaumont who would ask her for favours.

Rue Cambon was at the heart of the Paris fashion scene in the 1920s, with its boutiques and perfumers including those of Jeanne Paquin, Louis Cartier, Jean Patou and Charles Frederick Worth. Paul Morand recalled his first visit to Chanel's rue Cambon salon, for a New Year's Eve party in 1921. After Misia announced to a select crowd at Le Boeuf sur le Toit, 'You're all invited to Coco's', Chanel hastily arranged for a buffet to be set out in the fitting rooms.

Chanel chose to surround herself with the well-connected so that she could absorb their gossip and pick up on new trends from the city's highest denizens. 'Before me, couturiers hid away, like tailors, at the back of their shops, whereas I lived a modern life, I shared the habits, the tastes and the needs of those whom I dressed.' She befriended 'people of quality to act as a liaison between myself and society, between the inside and the outer world'.

After twelve years together, Misia and José-Maria Sert married in 1920, and they invited Gabrielle on their honeymoon to Italy, as a way of coaxing her out of mourning for Boy. 'I have seen her appear at the moment of my greatest grieving,' said Coco of Misia. 'Other people's grief lures her, just as certain fragrances lure the bee.'

At this time, Chanel was also grieving for her sister Antoinette. In November 1919 she had married a Canadian airman whom she had met in Paris during the victory celebrations marking the end of the First World War. He was from a modest family, but had led Antoinette to believe she was marrying into greater prosperity. In Canada she was deeply unhappy, writing to Chanel for money to help her return to France. Chanel refused, advising her to

Coco Chanel, Misia Sert and Hélène Berthelot sunbathing at the Lido in Venice, in 1925.

persevere, but instead Antoinette ran off to South America with an Argentinian man, where it is believed she either died of Spanish flu or committed suicide.

In Venice, Coco and Misia searched antique shops, spent evenings in salons and visited churches and chapels that gave spiritual comfort to Coco. She found Venice restorative, and Sert, with his obsession for, and knowledge of, art, addictive. He was 'the ideal travelling companion', said Gabrielle, as he would take them on excursions through Italy to find the most exquisite food, a secret local restaurant or to a palace with huge frescoes. 'Sert, who was lavish by nature, ordered rare wines, and meals that made our table look like a painting by Veronese or Parmigiano,' and would declare, 'I shall order another three zabagliones with maraschino cherries! Whether you want it or not!'[9]

Following Capel's marriage to Diana, Chanel lived in a ground-floor apartment at 46 quai Debilly, with views of the Seine and Trocadéro. It belonged to an opium-addict friend of Misia Sert's, and featured a large statue of Buddha, a black-lacquer

ceiling, a mirrored entrance hall and kimonos hanging in the closet. Chanel hired a butler, Joseph Leclerc, and he and his wife and daughter would go on to stay with her for fifteen years.[10] But on her return from Italy, Chanel wrote a telegram to Paris, ordering her belongings to be moved out. 'I didn't want to set foot in it again. When I went back to Paris, I moved into the Ritz again.' On the night table in her suite, she kept a tourist replica of the basilica of St Anthony of Padua, where she said she had experienced an awakening, seeing a man in complete despair, and realising her pain couldn't compare.

As well as keeping a room at the Ritz, after Boy's death, Coco retreated to La Milanaise, her rented home in the Paris suburb of Rueil, which had served as a secret love nest with Capel. But he was dead, and she asked for her bedroom to be painted black, with black sheets on her bed and black curtains draped from the window.[11] It was a tomb to her mourning, but it proved excessive and she chose to move to an art nouveau villa, Bel Respiro, on avenue Alphonse de Neuville, in Garches, a western suburb of Paris, in March 1920. The house was on a quiet road next door to that of Henri and Antoinette Bernstein and, in a twist, the home had formerly belonged to Boy Capel, as a place for his wife Diana and their daughter. Maybe living there helped Coco feel closer to Boy, serving as a place in which she could imagine being his wife.

Gabrielle believed that 'the interior of a home is the natural projection of a soul', and her soul was in pain. Despite the disapproval of her neighbours, she chose to paint the traditional shutters of Bel Respiro glossy black, and these contrasted with the beige of the exterior – the classic Chanel colour combination, which was replicated in the interior. She developed the home into a modernist sanctuary, where she could hide with her grief when not working at her salon.

In the summer of 1920, Chanel was photographed walking hand in hand with the Bernsteins' young daughter on the road outside their home. She was wearing a sports cape from her 1920 collection, inspired by American YMCA volunteers. She was also photographed with their daughter in her garden at Garches, wearing white pyjamas – a controversial item for women at the time. Henri Bernstein was also pictured in similar white pyjamas, an early example of a unisex piece of clothing.[12]

Clockwise from top
left: Igor Stravinsky,
José-Maria Sert, Coco
Chanel and Misia Sert
at the Paris Fair, 1920.

In May 1920, Chanel attended the Parisian premiere of the first postwar Diaghilev and Stravinsky ballet, *Pulcinella*, for which Picasso again designed the costumes and sets, reflecting the concept of fancy dress. The ballet launched Igor Stravinsky into fashionable Parisian circles, and a costume ball held by Prince Firouz of Persia followed the premiere, at which Chanel was introduced to the wonder composer. Chanel had been at the infamous opening night of *The Rite of Spring* in Paris, in 1913, a ballet that had been so shocking that it provoked a riot in the audience.

In the late summer of 1920, an impoverished Stravinsky returned to Paris with his wife Catherine and two children, who were all suffering illness. Always with a desire to help the struggling artist, Chanel offered for him to stay at Bel Respiro, as she would often be at the Ritz. By September 1920 he was living at Bel Respiro, having written a postcard to Swiss conductor Ernest Ansermet from that address on 22 September, stating that 'my nerves are in poor condition these days.'[13]

Stravinsky stayed at Chanel's until spring 1921, when he moved his family to the warmer Biarritz. The comfort of Bel Respiro must have been relaxing to his nerves, however, with Chanel as his benefactor, muse and lover. The restful atmosphere allowed him to finish his *Concertino for String Quartet*, the ballet, *Les noces*, and his Claude Debussy tribute, *Symphonies D'instruments à Vent*. He also created a series of compositions for the piano, *Les Cinq Doigts*, based on the number five – perhaps a link to his passion for Chanel.

Chanel was captivated by Russian émigrés Diaghilev and Stravinsky, and she became transfixed by another handsome Russian aristocrat who had escaped the revolution. In February 1921, Gabrielle was at a party at Marthe Davelli's when she met the Grand Duke Dmitri Pavlovich. As grandson to Tsar Nicholas II and cousin to Tsar Nicholas, his family was massacred by the Bolsheviks in 1918, and he narrowly escaped with his life having been present on the night Rasputin was murdered. Like other Romanovs in France, Dmitri was now penniless and living in Biarritz with Davelli, who offered him to Chanel in the summer of 1920, as he 'is a little expensive for me'.[14] Dmitri was eight years younger than Chanel, but she felt connected to him because his mother, Alexandra of Greece, also died when he was very young.

'Those Grand Dukes were all the same – they looked marvellous but there was nothing behind,' said Chanel. 'Green eyes, fine hands and shoulders, peace-loving, timorous. They drank so as not to be afraid. They were tall and handsome and splendid, but behind it all – nothing: just vodka and the void.'[15]

By spring 1921 Dmitri and Chanel were lovers, and she invited him to live with her in Garches. In return he may have bestowed on her Romanov pearls and gems, the few possessions with which he had fled Russia. Chanel was enraptured by these exquisite jewels, particularly a thirty-two-string pearl necklace that shaped her love for ropes and ropes of pearls, gilt chains and crosses.

The war had not only had a dramatic impact on women's clothing, but also on how the wealthy wore their jewels. It had been considered unpatriotic to flaunt jewellery under such hardship, so costume jewellery made a statement of style rather than wealth. Paul Poiret and Madeleine Vionnet were the first designers to incorporate costume jewellery in their collections, but it was Chanel who really made it chic, with her use of plexiglass and acrylic. In 1924, Chanel set up her own jewellery workshops, and Comte Étienne de Beaumont became her manager. Chanel's

Chanel and Grand
Duke Dmitri Pavlovich
of Russia, 1920.

first collection was based on the Byzantine and Renaissance periods, and included dramatic crosses encrusted with heavy stones. But her most famous design involved strings of faux pearls, and by 1925 everyone in Paris was wearing Chanel, or imitation Chanel, pearls. These pearls had a lustrous sheen, and the length of rope was designed to complement the silhouette of her gowns.

Vogue advised readers to wear large Chanel pearls in 'pink, blue, almond and grey', ensuring they wouldn't be mistaken for the real thing. Chanel created fake pearl chokers, brooches and earrings, which were made fashionable when worn by Lydia Sokolova, a principal dancer at Ballets Russes, while performing in the ballet *Le Train Bleu*. In 1926 Chanel also created a trend for asymmetrical earrings – with one black and one white pearl.

Chanel liked to break the rules of how to wear jewellery, piling them on during the day, and really paring them back for evening wear. Chanel told Haedrich: 'Nothing is more idiotic than confusing simplicity and poverty. I wonder how a suit cut out of the finest cloth, very meticulously finished, luxuriously lined, can look poor, especially when it's worn with the accessories I've made fashionable – the chains, the necklaces, the stones, the brooches, all the things that have enriched women so much and so cheaply, since they're imitation. Thanks to me they can walk around like millionaires.'[16]

The Ballets Russes toured Spain at the start of 1921, and Stravinsky asked Gabrielle to meet him there. Instead, she bought a new Silver Cloud Rolls-Royce convertible, and drove with Dmitri from Paris to the South of France, where they explored the hillside villages and winding roads high above the Riviera coastline. On their return to Paris, they passed the spot where Arthur had been killed, marked by a cross that Chanel had secretly commissioned. They then drove through Aix-en-Provence, taking a detour to Vichy, where she visited the places of her youth, including the Convent at Aubazine.[17]

When Misia found out Gabrielle was with Dmitri, she couldn't resist stirring, and sent a telegram to Stravinsky in Spain. 'Coco is a little shop girl who prefers Grand Dukes to artists,' it read. Gabrielle felt betrayed and refused to speak to Misia for some time, and it marked the end of the Stravinsky affair. However Chanel and Stravinsky did remain friends, with the designer acting as benefactor and sending him money frequently.[18]

Coco Chanel hired Russian aristocrats to run her business. Count Koutousov, formerly governor of Crimea, was the head receptionist at Chanel, and many of her sales girls, mannequins and seamstresses were young Russian women.

'I employed some of them; I have always felt immensely sorry for princes of royal blood; their job, when they are able to carry it out, is the saddest there is, and when they are unable to carry it out, that's worse. Furthermore, Russians fascinated me. Inside everyone from the Auvergne there is an Oriental one doesn't realise is there: the Russians revealed the Orient to me.'[19]

Chanel's affair with Dmitri introduced a strong Slavic essence to her designs, and the affair was later captured in Cuir de Russie, her 1927 perfume. The Grand Duchess Marie Pavlovna, Dmitri's sister, also played an important role in the shaping of Chanel's Russia collection. Marie met Chanel in Paris, in the autumn of 1921, and was impressed by her business sense. 'She had just then imported some multicoloured Faro Island sweaters and had conceived the idea of using their design for embroidery on silk blouses,' she said.

Marie was in the rue Cambon salon when she overheard an argument between Chanel's embroiderer, Madame Bataille, over the cost of embroidery on a crimson crepe de Chine blouse. Chanel refused to shift on the haggling of the price of the blouse, and after Madame Bataille left, Marie offered to do the embroidery for the price Chanel was asking. Marie spent a month training herself to machine embroider in a dingy workroom in Paris, and she established Kitmir, her embroidery business, in January 1922. Using patterns and designs from memories of her homeland, she sold the fabrics to Chanel, whose Russian collection was one of the most important of her career to date, and reflected the taste for the exotic after the First World War.

The Slavic influence inspired Chanel's designs for her collection in 1922, particularly in her use of velvet and folklore embroidery. Russian peasant clothing helped shape new silhouettes, such as a belted roubachka blouse made from silk crepe de Chine, a striped undershirt with a sailor's jacket, based on Russian military uniform, and a Hussar fur collection for Deauville. As British *Vogue* wrote in March 1922: 'Chanel lends oriental brilliance to black Crepe de Chine by Russian and Balkan embroideries.'[20]

As well as buying Marie's fabrics, Chanel also took it upon herself to shape her image, persuading her to lose weight and taking scissors to her hair one day. As Marie remembered in her memoir: 'Before I had time to realise what she was doing, she had pulled out my hairpins, snatched up the scissors and was cutting off my hair by the handful.'

It was in 1922 that Gabrielle began an affair with Pierre Reverdy, a friend of Picasso's and part of the group of artists who had gathered in Montmartre before the First World War. Misia was one of the first buyers of his obscure, self-published poetry, and supported his literary journal, *Nord-Sud*, which was named after the Montmartre to Montparnasse Métro line. The journal featured the leading figures of cubism and Dadaism, with illustrations by Fernand Léger, Georges Braque, Juan Gris and André Derain.

Reverdy's father was a Languedoc winemaker, and his earthy southern qualities appealed to Chanel, as he was country born, just as she was. Reverdy gifted Chanel with his signed books, rare first editions, with which she furnished her bookcases. 'Books have been my best friends. Just as the radio is a box full of lies, so each book is a treasure.'[21]

Despite his feelings for Chanel, Reverdy was married to a seamstress, Henriette, who stitched the binding of his first books, and continued to live in their Montmartre flat while Reverdy was living with Chanel. Typically a pessimist, Reverdy felt guilt over his affair, and with a deep spirituality and need for solitude, he joined the Abbey Saint-Pierre de Solesmes in 1925, with his wife joining the neighbouring convent. Gabrielle was devastated to lose him in this way, but they continued to stay in touch. He would later help her with the *bon mots* she gave French *Vogue* in 1938, such as 'women can give everything with a smile, and with a tear take it all back'.

Chanel celebrated turning forty in 1923, by moving from the Ritz and signing a long-term lease on the ground and first floors of the Hotel de Lauzun, an eighteenth-century townhouse at 29 rue du Faubourg Saint-Honoré. The apartment opened out onto formal gardens stretching to avenue Gabriel, the street where

Chanel on the back terrace of her apartment at 29 rue du Faubourg Saint-Honoré in 1929, modelling her popular pleated skirt and cardigan-style jacket.

once lived with Boy Capel. The home was owned by the Comte Pillet-Will, who remained on the floor above, and some of Paris's top designers held ateliers on the prestigious street. The *New York Times* described her apartment as being 'a famous old mansion whose history stretches far back into the eighteenth century. It housed many generations of eminent Parisians and is known today as the Hotel Montbazon Chabot. Its extensive gardens are even more beautiful than those of the neighbouring club running to the avenue Gabriel.'[22]

As well as being close to the popular private club Cercle interallié, Chanel's apartment backed on to Les Ambassadeurs nightspot on avenue Gabriel, and she was neighbours with the Rothschilds and the British Embassy. People would drift back and forth between these homes on the way to Les Ambassadeurs. As was noted in British weekly tabloid *The Bystander* in 1930, as a sly comment on Chanel's avant-garde circles: 'It would be quite exciting if some crashers from the Ambassadeurs tried to get into

Chanel's house through the back gates, or the British Embassy, for they might be hit over the head, as Coco Chanel only likes intelligent people, or at least people who write poetry.'

It was in this beautiful apartment on Faubourg Saint-Honoré, furnished as the epitome of Parisian elegance, that Chanel would establish herself as one of the most glamorous women in the world. Despite being critical of Misia's messy style, of her home with 'all that pile of objects', she asked Misia and Sert to help decorate the apartments. The interiors had been altered in the nineteenth century, and she loathed the green and gilt panelled walls, instead painting them in pale colours and covering them with ornate floor-to-ceiling mirrors.

Mixing modernism with Renaissance and Louis XIV pieces and Oriental style, the interiors were very contemporary 1920s. Chanel's taste continued to focus on black, beige and gold, with crystal pieces to bring light. She told Paul Morand, who was a guest at the home during the 1920s: 'Plush carpet everywhere, "colorado claro" in colour, with silky tints, like good cigars, woven to my specifications, and brown velvet curtains with gold braiding that looked like coronets girdled in yellow silk from Winston's. I never discussed prices; only my friends protested, and Misia pulled out her hair in despair.'[23]

She used her favoured Coromandel screens to create divides, she upholstered her *haute-époque* chairs with beige satin, and she placed comfortable sofas in the rooms, including a large orange velvet sofa. Two side tables, which were decorated with crystal-ball lamps and parchment lampshades, had been bought from Marchesa Luisa Casati, an eccentric who lived at the Ritz and had recently gone bankrupt. Rare editions filled the shelves of her library, which had a classic look, with natural wood, old carpets, beige furnishings and a marble torso bought on her trip to Italy with the Serts.

Chanel's bedroom also had large mirror panels, Coromandel screens, a huge Venetian mirror decorated with crystal flowers. Chanel's bed was enclosed with cream silk curtains, and had dark fur draped across it and a crystal chandelier hanging above. Chanel's intrigued guests often bribed the maid to show them Mademoiselle's room. 'I want to see what she sleeps in,' said Maurice de Rothschild. The room was empty and the bed

Inside Chanel's apartment at 29 rue du Faubourg Saint-Honoré.

was made, and he was surprised to find that under the covers were white cotton sheets.[24]

'People said of the way the place was furnished that it was in England that I learnt about luxurious decor. That's wrong; luxury, for me, meant the house of my uncle from Issoire, and that has remained with me: fine Auvergne furniture "polished by age", dark, heavy woods from the countryside, purple cherry wood, pear wood that was black beneath its sheen, rather like Spanish credence tables or Flemish sideboards, Boulle clocks in a tortoiseshell stand, cupboards with shelves that bent under the weight of clothes. I had thought that my childhood was a modest one, but I realise it was sumptuous. In Auvergne, everything was real, everything was big.'[25]

The home was staffed with a cook, maids and footmen, hired by Joseph, her faithful butler, to create a palace of entertainment. It was one of the most sociable periods of Chanel's life, playing the hostess at wonderful, stylish parties to mark cultural events such as the closing of the Ballets Russes season, with the finest champagne and caviar, her gardens lit by lanterns, and a guest list of the cream of Paris society and avant-garde artists. One evening Chanel invited African-American singer Florence Mills and the Blackbirds to perform at her salon, with the jazz band set up in the garden. Stravinsky, Diaghilev and the Ballets Russes pianist would play on her grand piano in the evenings, which was one of her first purchases for the home. When Pillet-Will complained of the noise, she offered to pay him for the entire townhouse, and he agreed to move out.[26]

Gabrielle set aside a room for Picasso, who hated staying in his villa outside Paris and preferred to be in the city with its noise and company. Gabrielle had been one of the select guests at his wedding in 1918, when wife Olga wore a Chanel white satin and tulle gown, described by Cocteau as 'very Biarritz'. Chanel was 'seized by a passion' for Picasso. She said 'he was wicked. He fascinated me the way a hawk would; he filled me with a fear. I could feel it when he came in: something would curl up in me; he'd arrived. I couldn't see him yet, but already I knew he was in the room.'[27]

The 1920s marked the period during which Chanel's signature style was first conceived and she set the trends for women. Paul

Left: Marquise de Jaucourt in a Chanel wool dress and matching coat in Biarritz, photographed by George Hoyningen-Huene, 1927.

Right: Actress Ina Claire, photographed by *Vogue* in 1924 in the Chanel sportswear look of herringbone tweed skirt and sweater.

Poiret said: 'What has Chanel invented? Poverty de luxe. Formerly women were architectural, like the prows of ships, and very beautiful. Now they resemble little undernourished telegraph clerks.'

The decade saw hem lengths rise and fall, but Chanel chose to keep the hem just below the knee, which suited the new generation of active, modern women in pursuit of freedom, tanning their skin and throwing their bodies into energetic dances. The 1921 *garçonne* look was led by Chanel's sporty

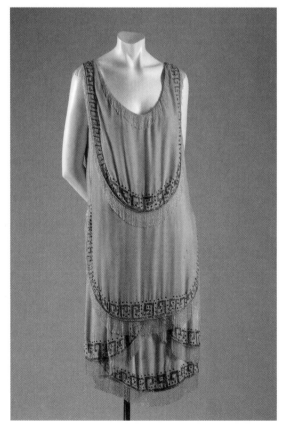

**Above left: Silk crepe
evening cape, 1927.**

**Above left: Silk crepe
evening cape, 1927.**

**Above right: Dancer and
choreographer Desiree
Lubovska wearing a
multitiered sequinned
Chanel dress with a
square decolletage,
photographed for
Vogue, 1925.**

**Below right: Evening
gown, silk velvet with
rhinestone and glass
bead details, 1926.**

**Below left: Marion
Morehouse wearing a
white crepe Chanel
dress with wrap bodice
and silk fringe on the
skirt, photographed
for *Vogue*, 1926.**

skirts, dropped waistlines, and cloche hats resting on short hair. Marquis Boni de Castellane said: 'Women no longer exist; all that's left are the boys created by Chanel.' In March 1923, *Vogue* wrote that 'Gabrielle Chanel is now famous for her treatment of the youthful short-skirted silhouette which innumerable smart women have achieved.'

The *garçonne* look took dedication to achieve, and *Vogue* described the hours women spent at the gym, the pills they took and the 'rubber girdles' for creating the slender ideal. Chanel's dresses may have led the way for ridding the world of corsets, but it was difficult to achieve the desired figure without one. Despite the high maintenance required for these clothes, Chanel's designs were practical – her travel coats were easy to wear, with big pockets to replace bags, sweaters with four buttons at the front for easy fastening, and foldable hats for fitting into a case.[28]

Another signature element was the camellia flower, likely first incorporated in 1922 as embroidery on a blouse, and then added in fabric form as an embellishment. The flower was associated with the *demimonde* and *La Dame aux Camélias*, which had so entranced Chanel as a girl, and where the camellia marked a woman who could be seduced. 'In America they used to send me orchids before dinner and I used to say put them in the ice-box. Imagine wearing something that dies on you – if I wear a flower it's an artificial one.'

In 1923 beige and red were Chanel's favoured colour combination, often used in geometric designs, and evident in her interiors. 'I take refuge in beige because it's natural,' she said. 'Not dyed. Red, it's the colour of blood and we've so much inside us it's only right to show a little outside.' Evening gowns were in beige, rose pink and burgundy, decorated with camellia pins and silk floral corsages. Other colours included dark green, grey, navy blue, white and black.

The modernism and bohemian creativity of the first half of the decade all came together at the 1925 Paris Exposition, where the newly conceived art deco movement launched Paris as the centre of design, jazz and excitement. The French pavilion at the exposition featured a smoking room in black lacquer, with exotic red and silver embellishments, and this contrast of black with orange, red and gilt defined the Orientalism of art deco design.

The 1926 Little Black Dress, which Vogue hailed as the fashion equivalent of the Ford motorcar.

In 1926 Coco Chanel's little black dress was heralded as the essential item for the smart woman's wardrobe. It was called 'little' because it was discreet, and in October 1926, American *Vogue* hailed it as the fashion equivalent of the Ford motorcar, which had been revolutionary in the twenties. They wrote 'The Chanel "Ford" – the frock that all the world will wear – is model "817" of black crepe de Chine. The bodice blouses slightly at (the) front and sides and has a tight bolero at the back. Especially chic is the arrangement of tiny tucks which cross in front; imported by Saks Fifth Avenue.' This frock, which was sketched in *Vogue*, was a simple black crepe de Chine sheath dress with long narrow sleeves. Acting as a canvas for the string of white pearls, it allowed women to dictate their own silhouette, rather than being pinched and squeezed into shape.[29]

This dress made a huge impact, but the colour wasn't novel for Chanel – she had used black in her collections since 1917. Coco appreciated the contrast of black and white, or black against beige, which perhaps reminded her of her convent uniform, and the corridor that she trailed along every day as a child. She told Paul Morand: 'Women think of every colour, except the absence of colours. I have said that black had everything. White too. They have an absolute beauty. It is perfect harmony. Dress women in white or black at a ball: they are the only ones you see.'[30]

She declared that 'before me no one would have dared to dress in black'. Black was still considered the colour of mourning, too dramatic to be worn entirely during the day or at night. When Boy Capel died, she had turned her home into a mausoleum with black shutters, but Chanel dismissed the rumours that she chose black in fashion because of her despair. 'Elsa Maxwell wrote in a New York newspaper that since I couldn't wear mourning for Boy Capel because I hadn't been married to him, I was making the whole world wear it. What bad taste.'[31]

She herself said she was given the idea for black in 1920, at a charity event at the opera called the *Bal des Petits Lits Blancs*, when she looked down from the balcony at a sea of women in gaudy colours. She told her companion, 'These colours are impossible. These women, I'm bloody well going to dress them in black! So I imposed black ... Black wipes out everything ...'[32]

Black became the chicest colour, and from 1926 her day dresses were made from wool or marocain, and evening dresses in silk crepe, velvet and satin. Black lace dresses were threaded with beige metal, or with gold lace and turquoise or coral beads. It was the simple elegance of black that made them the perfect backdrop for her costume jewellery. 'For four or five years I made only black,' she said. 'My dresses sold like mad with little touches – a white collar, or cuffs. Everyone wore them – actresses, society women, housemaids.'[33]

Chanel was caught up in work, her business consumed her, and she enjoyed her circle of friends. As well as being the decade's most exciting designer, creatively she felt accepted by the avant-garde when she was invited to design costumes for Jean Cocteau's 1922 adaption of *Antigone*, which also featured sets designed by Picasso. Cocteau chose Chanel because 'she is the greatest couturière of our age, and it is impossible to imagine the daughters of Oedipus poorly dressed'.

In 1924 Chanel designed for the avant-garde dance performances *Les Soirées de Paris*, with Cocteau, Picasso and Jean Hugo amongst others, and in 1926 Cocteau again asked her to create costumes for the 1926 production of *Orpheus*. She also helped to fund a 1927 production of *Oedipus Rex* by Stravinsky and Diaghilev.

Chanel was Paris, and Paris was Chanel. She said: 'Fashion in a country's style should reflect the way people live, the way people dress in that country. Here everyone does everything he can to prevent Frenchwomen from dressing the way one dresses in France.' But through the influence of one of the wealthiest men in Europe, the Duke of Westminster, she also introduced another element into her designs.

4

Rue Cambon

'Screens were the first thing I ever bought. You don't come across them much in the provinces, of course. I'd never seen anything like it...'

Paris
1918–1971

Towards the end of 1918, Coco Chanel signed a lease for 31 rue Cambon, where she registered for the first time in Paris as a couturière rather than a milliner. The building was set over five floors and it featured a boutique, a workroom, a salon for high-profile clients and Chanel's own private apartment with three rooms – a hall, living room and dining room. Later on she would add a mirrored bathroom. Scented with Chanel N°.5 and traces of cigarette smoke, it would be a gathering place for the most influential people in Paris, all keen to experience Chanel and her style.

To add to her collection of properties on rue Cambon, which included the original number 21, she would later acquire numbers 27 and 29, which she used for her workrooms. In 1929, Chanel also opened an accessories boutique on rue Cambon, where she sold scarves and wool jersey caps, perfumes and a beauty line that included red lipstick, a face cream in 1927, and self-bronzing lotion L'Huile Tan in 1932.[117]

Chanel's private apartment reflected her bohemian tastes, the rooms filled with many different pieces that had meaning to her: Coromandel screens; Louis XIV furniture; eighteenth-century Venetian mirrors; smoked crystal and amethyst to reflect purity and light; wood or alabaster animals, that included life-sized deer and bronze lions; shelves crammed with rare books; a Mongolian meteorite; and a statue of the Virgin and Child. Beige was Chanel's signature colour, but it was never dull – gold-painted silk on the walls, luxury beige carpets and soft beige sofas. She ensured there were vases of white flowers – lilies and tuberoses – around the boutique and apartment.

The rue Cambon interiors reflected the interior decoration of Chanel's early apartment on avenue Gabriel, the setting of her love affair with Boy Capel, and all her homes in Paris would follow a similar style. Boy had shaped her desire for Coromandel screens, white flowers, shelves crammed with books and Chinese furniture, and she combined this with elements influenced by her friends, the Serts – Venetian figurines and baroque wall features.

Chanel in 1937 with her beloved Coromandel screens, which defined her interior decoration style.

Chanel in her apartment
at 31 rue Cambon in
the late 1950s.

She sometimes took apart Coromandel screens, converting them
into low coffee tables or plastering their wooden panels onto the
walls of her entrance hall.

In 1921, Chanel commissioned a crystal chandelier, with
smoked crystal and amethyst fruits and flowers, metal number
'5's, and the initials 'B', for Boy Capel, and 'C' for Coco Chanel.
She brought back mirrors from her trip to Venice, later discovering
they'd once been part of the treasures of a church in Seville. She
acquired a meterorite, which she rested on marble, and she
placed a fifth-century Greek marble torso on her mantelpiece,
doubled by its reflection in the Louis XIV mirror, and flanked by
Italian baroque boiserie.

Chanel also believed in duality – behind the beige sofa at rue
Cambon there were two horses, two camels and two frogs. The

Left: Smoked crystal chandelier, designed by Baccarat in 1921.

Right: Wheat was a strong theme in Chanel's home, captured in bronze with this coffee table, and with dried sheaths of wheat in a vase.

lion emblem helped her heal after Boy's death, as she saw it everywhere on her recovery trip to Venice with the Serts, and she kept a pair of gold lions on the coffee table by her sofa. She also kept a rock-crystal sphere on a plinth with three lions, made by the goldsmith Robert Goossens.

Wheat was another symbol that Chanel chose in her life, as it reminded her of her father and represented a good harvest. She displayed natural sheaths and ears of wheat in vases, replacing it annually, and she kept artificial wheat in bronze, wood or rock crystal. When Salvador Dalí offered to paint for her, Chanel asked for sheathes of wheat, and he depicted it on a black background. The painting was hung by the bookshelves behind her beige sofa at rue Cambon.

New objects would be added to the apartment over the years, some coming from her French Riviera property La Pausa or from the apartment at rue du Faubourg Saint-Honoré. But pride of place at rue Cambon were the pieces that were most precious to her – the meteorite, Paul Reverdy's books, and all those things that reminded her of Boy.

Chanel on the mirrored staircase of her salon at 31 rue Cambon, where she held her shows.

The eclectic objects of Chanel's apartment, including the twin deers, statue of Aphrodite and petrified tree on the mantelpiece, in 1956.

Her rue Cambon apartment retained the sense of a magical space, or an 'Ali Baba's cave', as Marcel Haedrich described it. He wrote of it as a vision of 'Byzantium and the imperial palace of China, Ptolemy's Egypt, and, in the mirrors above the fireplace, reflections of Greece with a fourth-century Aphrodite side by side with a fantastic raging wild boar, a meteorite that had fallen from the sky on Mongolia thousands of years ago – everything agglomerated and conglomerated, mingled and mangled, ordered into a disorder magnificently made harmonious by Coco's taste'.[118]

In a piece she wrote on Chanel for the *New Yorker* in 1931, American journalist Janet Flanner described rue Cambon: 'Where other establishments indulge in tapestries and *objets d'art* as furnishings, serve cocktails to buyers, and display their mannequins on a stage, No. 31, rue Cambon looks neither like a museum, a bar, nor a revue. It looks what it is, a shop – deluxe and glassy, but still a shop. Upstairs and behind the glass scenes it is a rabbit warren of corkscrew staircases, labyrinthine corridors, and sodden doors.'[119]

Chanel's mirrored salon created the sense of an endless space, and it was a place of complete modernity – it was sleek, functional and art deco. Chanel installed a mirrored staircase in 1928, which led from the ground floor to her private apartments. It offered a multidimensional view of her salon, a fractured reflection of the many women seated to watch her show, or admiring themselves in Chanel gowns. Chanel would tell her friend Claude Delay, 'I spent my life on stairs,' and perhaps this staircase in the salon reminded her of the stone steps at Aubazine.

The mirrors were in place when *Vogue* editor Bettina Ballard, as a student in Paris in the 1920s, applied to be a Chanel mannequin to earn extra money. 'I read an advertisement in the Paris *Herald* that Chanel wanted American mannequins. I put on my hat and went to the rue Cambon to offer myself … when I reached the top of Chanel's mirrored stairs, I wasn't quite so confident. *Vendeuses* in black dresses were rushing around with clothes over their arms and I couldn't stop anyone to tell them what I had come for. The salon, with its big Coromandel screens, was filled with customers watching tall Russian mannequins moving around in a bored, slouched way showing very *décolleté* knee-length balldresses. The air smelled like a million gardenias. The room looked enormous.'[120]

While unsuccessful as a model, Bettina Ballard often visited Chanel as *Vogue*'s Paris fashion editor from the mid-thirties, and she was always impressed by the upstairs apartment, describing being 'shielded by tall Coromandel screens and surrounded by pieces of carved gilded wood, books to the ceiling, bronze *doré* lions and other animals in jade and terra-cotta, and furniture covered in beige suede. There was a wood fire burning which, with all the gold and bronze and beige, gave the room a golden glow pierced by Chanel's darting black eyes ... I love this room, which grows more richly Chanel every year as she adds treasures to it and more and more pairs of glasses, which she can pick up wherever she is standing. Sometimes I feel that Coco is in the room when she isn't – it is so full of the sound of her words, of her scent, of her very being.'[121]

Chanel found that her ideas came to her when relaxing on her large beige suede sofa in the rue Cambon drawing room, lit by the gentle glow from the fireplace. When it came to designing jewellery, she would sit in comfort, toying with a mix of jewels she kept on top of her coffee table adapted from a Coromandel screen. She set the stones into a soft piece of mouldable plastic, flattening it on the table and, creating designs from real gems and fakes, she studied the overall effect of how they looked together – Thai rubies, topaz, which she described as 'golden water', paste stones and sapphires.[122]

'I've made my best journeys on my couch,' she said. She didn't so much like travel as she liked the idea of escaping, and so she found she could visit far-off places just by lying on her sofa, with her objects reminding her of the places she'd seen, and of the people who had impacted on her life.

The sofa in the apartment at rue Cambon was where Chanel would relax and entertain.

5 The Scent of Success

'Women wear the perfumes they're given as presents. You ought to wear your own, the one you like. If I leave a jacket behind somewhere, they know it's mine.'

Grasse
1920

While it is considered a classic symbol of refined taste, in the twenties, Chanel N°.5 was the scent of *la garçonne*, enveloping her as she danced the Charleston, sipped cocktails and embraced the avant-garde. With her short hair, her groundbreaking style, her lovers, her lifestyle, Chanel was the epitome of what the flapper hoped to achieve, and Chanel N°.5 was her scent. The cartoonist Sem created an illustration for the perfume's, showing a modern 1920s woman reaching out for a bottle of Chanel N°.5.[1]

Chanel had been thinking of creating her own scent for some time, and in Monte Carlo in 1920, she met perfumer Ernest Beaux. Born in Moscow, to a French father, Beaux had been master perfumer at Russia's Rallet & Co, perfume company to the Imperial Court, but he had settled in France following the 1918 revolution. He set up a laboratory in Grasse, the perfume capital of France, surrounded by vast fields of unique, fragrant flowers.

Chanel was looking for a scent that blended different floral notes, rather than the traditional single note, and could be worn like a satin gown, lingering on the skin. 'I, who love woman, wanted to give her clothes in which she could be comfortable, in which she could drive a car, yet at the same time clothes that emphasised her femininity, clothes that flowed with her body. A woman is closest to being naked when she is well dressed. I wanted to give her a perfume, but an artificial perfume … I don't want rose or lily of the valley; I want a perfume that is compound,' she said.[2]

Beaux was an experimenter of synthetic aldehydes, which enhanced the ingredients and let the essence stay on the skin for longer. Benzyl acetate worked particularly well with jasmine, making it a long-lasting scent. Beaux worked up ten different samples and presented each of them to Chanel in numerical order.

She chose a perfume that combined Grasse jasmine, ylang-ylang, neroli, May rose, sandalwood, Bourbon vetiver, and which was the fifth sample – no.5 – her magical number, to bring luck. She always presented her couture collections on the fifth day of

The 1921 illustration for Chanel N°.5, by cartoonist Sem (Georges Goursat).

the month, her star sign Leo was the fifth in the zodiac, and she also referenced the quintessence of old alchemists.

In an article in 1946, Beaux recounted: 'I went to present her with my creations – two series: 1 to 5 and 20 to 24. From these she chose several, including one labelled Number 5, and when I asked "What name should be given to it?", Mademoiselle Chanel replied: "I present my dress collection on the 5th of May, the fifth month of the year; we shall thus leave the number with which it is labelled and this number 5 shall bring it good luck.'[3] With complete luxury in mind, she wanted it to be the world's most expensive perfume, and asked for more jasmine from Grasse. For just one bottle, the exclusive recipe used one thousand Pégomas jasmine flowers and twelve Pégomas roses.[4]

After selecting the sample, Chanel took a vial to an exclusive Cannes restaurant, and as she dined with Beaux, she sprayed the perfume every time a stylish lady walked past. When they immediately looked around, intrigued at where the scent came from, she knew she had a success. By early 1921, Chanel N°.5 was in production and Coco returned to Paris with one hundred bottles in her luggage. She asked her sales girls to spray the perfume in the salon and fitting rooms, and sample bottles were given to her most influential clients, with only the vaguest notion of where they came

PARFUMS CHANEL

THE GIFT OF GOOD TASTE

from. The word on Chanel's mysterious scent was out, and with that perfect marketing campaign, it became the must-have perfume in Paris. In a rare black and beige catalogue from the early twenties, Chanel promoted the elite luxury fragrance as 'created exclusively for a clientele of connoisseurs', promoting the notion that it was only for refined tastes.[5]

The classic design of the glass bottle, possibly created with designer Maurice Depinoix, known for his artistry in perfume bottles, reflected Chanel's practical, unfussy ethos. It was the antithesis of the ornate, decorative perfume bottles of the time, with their flowering art nouveau stoppers. Chanel's bottle was more akin to masculine tastes, and one story on the design was that she had copied one of Arthur Capel's toiletry containers when commissioning the design, as it bore a strong resemblance to a medicine bottle. Chanel's bottle was also cubist in its shape, reminiscent of the octagonal Place Vendôme, which she could view from the window of her suite at the Ritz.

Left: A 1923 caricature by Sem of Chanel imagined as La Marquise de la Flaconnerie inside her perfume bottle in *Le Nouvelle Monde*.

Right: Misia Godebska-Natanson (Sert), by Félix Edouard Vallotton, 1898. Misia claimed to have discovered an ancient recipe that inspired Chanel N°.5.

In her memoirs, Misia Sert took credit for the invention of Chanel N°.5. Lucien Daudet, secretary to the Empress Eugénie, wife of Napoleon III, had been going through the empress's papers, and discovered a sixteenth-century beauty formula belonging to Queen Catherine de Medici, known as The Secret of the Medici, which was said to be an anti-ageing toilet water. Daudet bestowed the recipe on Misia, and she claimed she then took it to Gabrielle, suggesting they use this recipe as a basis for a perfume.

Of the design of the bottle, Misia said they 'painstakingly experiment(ed) with a very severe bottle, ultra-simple, almost pharmaceutical, but in the Chanel style and with the elegant touch she gave to everything'.[6]

From its launch, the bottle's stopper was emblazoned with the now iconic, double C logo, which could possibly have been a tribute to the memory of Arthur Capel. While the interlocking Cs were the initials for Coco Chanel, they were also representative of Capel and Chanel. Intertwined Cs were also evident on the 'Arthur Capel Cup' at the Paris Polo Club, where Arthur had played, and which was given to the club by his sister in collaboration with Gabrielle, not long after Arthur's death.[7]

The perfume sold well, but Chanel wanted to increase production for sales in department stores. It was impossible for Ernest Beaux to supply such quantities, so the owner of Galeries Lafayette, Théophile Bader, set up a meeting with cosmetics giant Pierre Wertheimer at the Longchamp racetrack. This racetrack deal led to the founding of Les Parfums Chanel in April 1924, with Chanel owning ten per cent of the company, the Wertheimers owning 70 per cent, and 20 per cent going to Bader.

In 1922 Chanel introduced her 'N°.22' perfume, with its name coming from its year of launch and from the number having a special meaning to her. Both she and Boy liked the number 2, and tragically, he had been killed at 2a.m. on 22 December. She worked with Ernest Beaux on further perfumes including Gardénia in 1925, Bois des Îles in 1928, and Cuir de Russie, in tribute to her Russian lovers, in 1927.

Chanel's perfumes made her incredibly wealthy and, for her, perfume was one of the most important ways for a woman to make an impression. 'One grows used to ugliness, but never slovenliness. Slovenliness in a woman means being neither perfumed nor washed. I am very fond of perfume. I like women who are well turned out and perfumed. It's degrading when they smell of slovenliness.'[8]

In anticipation of Chanel sweeping into rue Cambon every day, an assistant would spray N°.5 in the salon and on the staircase. It was also sprayed on the coals in the fireplace, heating up and filling the room with delicious scent. She told her friend and biographer Claude Delay: 'Women wear the perfumes they're given as presents. You ought to wear your own, the one you like. If I leave a jacket behind somewhere, they know it's mine. When I was young, the first thing I'd have done if I had any money was buy some perfume. I'd been given Floris's Sweet Peas – I thought it was lovely, country girl that I was. Then I realised it didn't suit me.' Her advice on perfume, according to Bettina Ballard, would be: 'Spray it on wherever you expect to be kissed – any woman who goes to excess in perfuming herself has no future because she will only offend her friends and admirers.'[9]

The British Look

'I brought in tweeds from Scotland; home-spuns came to oust crepes and muslins. I arranged for woollens to be washed less, so that they kept their softness; in France we wash too much.'

London, Cheshire and the Scottish Highlands
1924–1931

Edmonde Charles-Roux, one-time editor-in-chief of French *Vogue*, noted that 'from 1926 to 1931, the Chanel style was English', and the man who influenced this style was Hugh Grosvenor, the 2nd Duke of Westminster. Chanel was first introduced to an upper-crust sense of style through Boy Capel. He had once brought her to an English tailor who created luxurious versions of the alpaca suit and goatskin jacket she wore when she first arrived in Paris, and she said, 'everything to do with the rue Cambon stemmed from there'.[1] She was entranced by the rules of society she experienced with Boy's circle of polo-playing, public school friends, as well as the moneyed ladies who regularly visited her boutiques. Lady Iya Abdy, a socialite model and friend of Chanel's, wrote: 'Coco has always been impressed with money and titles. She, who overcame all life's barriers, was ashamed of her roots. Instead of being proud of where she came from, she tried fiercely to hide her origins. She vanquished everything except her childhood.'[2]

Chanel also admired how British aristocrats were understated in the way they dressed. They passed tweed coats along the generations, and the polished shoes, good-quality hunting clothes and pressed staff uniforms really appealed to her imagination. She said Westminster was 'elegance itself, he never has anything new; I was obliged to go and buy him some shoes, and he's been wearing the same jackets for twenty-five years'.[3] As the richest man in Britain, and maybe Europe, he lived a life of opulence, of ritual, of ensuring the coal fires were always burning in his homes, as he felt it was his duty as a landowner to keep coal miners in work. She learned the British customs of afternoon teas, outdoor sports, of cold manor houses and of dressing appropriately according to the seasons.

The Duke of Westminster was nicknamed Bendor, after one of his grandfather's thoroughbreds. Westminster had served alongside Winston Churchill in the Boer War, and they remained close friends as well as being related through marriage. Churchill's mother was married to Westminster's brother-in-law. In

Coco Chanel with Hugh Grosvenor, 2nd Duke of Westminster, at the Grand National in March 1925.

a quirk of fate, Coco and Westminster were also linked through marriage. Diana Capel, Boy's wife, had first been married to Westminster's half-brother Percy Wyndham, a union cut short when Percy died during the First World War.

Westminster married Constance Edwina Lewis in 1901, and their daughter Ursula was born in 1902, followed by a son, Edward. But they suffered tragedy in 1909 when four-year-old Edward died from appendicitis. Another daughter, Mary, was born in 1910, but grief drove a wedge through the marriage, and Westminster embarked on affairs with stage star Gertie Millar and ballerina Anna Pavlova. Because he had two daughters who would not inherit, Westminster needed a son to pass his vast wealth to. He married again, this time to Violet Nelson, a society belle, but she failed to produce this much desired heir.

During his marriage to Violet, Westminster purchased the *Flying Cloud*, one of the world's largest private yachts, which required a forty-man crew. The name was perhaps inspired by the heavenly white sails and white wooden deck, contrasting with the deep black of the hull. It was a colour scheme that Chanel would approve of. 'This is a most attractive yacht,' Winston Churchill wrote to wife Clementine in August 1923. 'Imagine a large four-masted cargo boat, fitted up in carved oak like a little country house, with front doors, staircases & lovely pictures. She can sail 12 knots and motor 8, & accommodate 16 guests.'[4]

Chanel was first introduced to the Duke of Westminster through her friend Vera Arkwright, who had been raised by aristocracy and was frequently in the company of the Prince of Wales and other royalty. In 1916, Vera married an American officer, Fred Bate, and they had a daughter together, but Vera was often away from her family in favour of enjoying the high life. The lifestyle of the rich and famous didn't quite match her income, and so she was employed by Chanel as a brand ambassador to model the latest designs.

Gabrielle and Vera spent Christmas and New Year 1923/1924 in Monte Carlo, where they stayed at the Hôtel de Paris. The *Flying Cloud* was moored in the harbour, and the Duke begged Vera to invite Coco Chanel to join him onboard. Gabrielle eventually agreed, however once she received a telegram that Dmitri was arriving in Monte Carlo, she swiftly cancelled her date with

Westminster. Dmitri was intrigued to experience the famous yacht, and so the dinner invitation was extended to him. They spent their evening being waited on by the numerous deckhands as the conversation flowed to the strains of a gypsy band, the deck illuminated by Christmas lights. After supper they were taken ashore for dancing and gambling at Monte Carlo Casino.

It was a romantic night and Westminster was desperate to see the vibrant designer again. Recently separated, he was now England's most eligible bachelor and he was impressed that she was a self-made woman. For Chanel it was simply that 'Westminster liked me because I was French. English women are possessive and cold. Men get bored with them.'

He flooded her apartment in Paris with fresh-cut flowers, baskets of fruit from his estate in Cheshire and fresh salmon flown directly to Paris from his rivers in Scotland. Chanel was devoted to her work, and she enjoyed her circle of artist friends – Jean Cocteau, Pablo Picasso, Serge Lifar and the Serts. She didn't think she had time for this man, obsessed with life's pleasures. Chanel was avant-garde, Westminster was old-world, but he escorted her to the opera, and during the dress rehearsal for the ballet *Le Train Bleu*, he was by her side. As well as boxes with orchids and camellias from his Eaton hothouses, Bendor casually bestowed huge gems on Chanel. When he sent her a box of fresh vegetables from his farm in Cheshire, her butler discovered, at the bottom, a large rough-cut emerald in a velvet box. 'He was so rich that he completely forgot about it,' Coco said. 'No thoughts of money ever influenced any of his reactions, his acts, his thoughts. He was never calculating.'[5]

In Paris, Westminster kept a permanent suite at the Hôtel Lotti, but the Duke of Westminster's seat was at Eaton Hall, a Gothic mansion in the Cheshire countryside. It was so enormous that he referred to it as 'St Pancras station'. His grandfather had designed the home, and it possessed an imposing medieval air, with a panelled dining room in which Gainsborough family portraits hung on the wall alongside priceless paintings that included the *Adoration of the Magi* by Rubens, and suits of armour flanked huge staircases. Ten housemaids serviced the estate, constantly cleaning up after the Duke's dachshunds, while thirty-eight gardeners tended the grounds. As Chanel described, there were

greenhouses 'as big as those that belong to the city of Paris. They grew food for every season – peaches, nectarines, strawberries...' and she was impressed that, in Chester, 'the prizes at the cattle shows were cheeses the size of this table'.[6]

Chanel was struck by the estate's setting, 'full of black and white half-timbered houses with pointed gables from the time of Falstaff ... it is surrounded by Italian-style terraces, training routes for horses from the studs, model farms, forests of rhododendrons as in the novel of Disraeli, and galleries where the Rubens, the Raphaels, the English masters and the Thorvaldsens are all the rage'.[7]

Chanel was particularly impressed by the cleanliness of Eaton Hall, reminiscent of her time at Aubazine. 'What you had to admire was the flawless order of that house, its English unaffectedness. It made you forget the ugly bits. A knight in armour stuck into a corner of a staircase, that does look a little overdone – unless it has always been there. Then you see it as something that grew out of the earth, proud and straight, especially when the armour is all shiny and looks ready for action.'[8]

Whenever Chanel accompanied Westminster to his estates, he was further captivated by her vigour, her sporting prowess and her riding skills. She was invited to join the boar hunt at Château de Woolsack, his Tudor-style mansion in Mimizan, on France's Atlantic coast, and she was always dressed appropriately for the occasion. She was also enthralled by the customs of the region. 'At Mimizan, when the boar had been killed, there was a delicious smell: the scent of tuberoses growing on sand,' she said. 'It's with the male sexual organs, not the female, that the best perfumes are made. Vibrant, full of life.' She also noted the traditions of Mimizan, where 'there were still men walking on stilts and knitting great thick woollen stockings'.[9]

Chanel was so enchanted by the region that she bought her own property in Mimizan, at 59 rue de la Poste, which served as an annual beach retreat for her seamstresses. In one of the first examples of paid holiday leave in France, Chanel's workers stayed in the cottage in shared rooms, where they washed from a pump in the garden, and could take a short walk down to the wide stretch of sandy beach.[10]

Winston Churchill enjoyed the boar hunting in Mimizan and he wrote to his wife Clementine: 'The famous Coco turned up & I took a great fancy to her – a most capable & agreeable woman – much the strongest personality Bennie has yet been up against. She hunted vigorously all day, motored to Paris after dinner & is today engaged in passing and improving dresses on endless streams of mannequins. Altogether 200 models have been settled in almost 3 weeks. Some have been altered ten times. She does it with her own fingers, pinning, cutting, looping, etc.'[11]

Besides Eaton Hall and Mimizan, other houses belonging to Westminster included a château near Deauville, a townhouse in Mayfair, London, and a huge swath of land in the north of

Previous page: Eaton Hall, the Duke of Westminster's seat in Cheshire, in 1911.

Scotland. Coco enjoyed the ritual of travelling by luxury train to the Westminster properties, where two Pullman cars and four baggage cars were occupied by the many pieces of luggage and his dogs.

Chanel discovered life with Westminster was an 'absurd fairyland', where everything was set up for guests, 'where you can dine and go to bed on your arrival, with polished silverware, motor cars (I can still see the seventeen ancient Rolls in the garage at Eaton Hall!) with their batteries charged, small tankers in the harbour, fully laden with petrol, servants in livery, stewards and, on the entrance table, always scattered everywhere, newspapers, magazines and journals from all over the world'.[12]

Westminster's greatest contentment was sailing, and while Chanel wasn't a fan of the sea, and didn't see the point of just staring out at the horizon for hours, the luxury seafaring lifestyle certainly appealed. 'Westminster owns two yachts: a Royal Navy

Chanel on the Duke of Westminster's boar hunt in Mimizan with Randolph and Winston Churchill.

reserve destroyer and a four-master,' she said. 'When you arrive on dry land, all the guests are wearing splendid yachting caps to go and buy postcards in the port. He never disembarks except in an old soft hat.'[13]

She chose navy blue for many designs and copied the twill pea coats and yachting caps of the *Flying Cloud* crew, adding gold buttons to the coat and a brooch to the cap. In 1926, *Vogue* was inspired by the *Flying Cloud* for a feature on yacht style, showcasing pleated jersey dresses that suited life lounging on decks.

Westminster travelled to Scotland on his destroyer, *The Cutty Sark*, as it was a long journey on rough roads to access the remote Sutherland region. The 100,000-acre Reay Forest estate in the rugged northwest of Scotland was originally leased by the 1st Duke of Westminster in 1866 from the Duke of Sutherland, his father-in-law, and Bendor, the 2nd Duke of Westminster, bought it in 1920. This area of the Highlands became his playground, where he held hunting parties and fished for salmon in the bountiful rivers.

One of Westminster's properties was Lochmore Lodge, a fifty-two-room granite mansion with Victorian Gothic turrets resting on the edge of the loch, and which offered beautiful mountain views. Stack Lodge was the Duke's sport's house on the River Laxford, wood-panelled and with stag antlers above the roaring fireplace. The bedrooms lay under the eaves, a space that may have brought back fond memories for Chanel of when she lived in an attic room. The lodge was only accessible by a storybook stone bridge over the river. Chanel fully embraced the country sports she was introduced to by Westminster, and reflected that 'on the moors of Scotland, the grouse are ready to be shot, or the salmon to be fished …'[14]

Author Justine Picardie discovered the leather-bound volumes of fishing records in the Reay estate office, where Chanel's fishing prowess has been forever recorded. Her name first appeared on 27 May 1925, with details of her 9lb salmon catch. She spent the summer of 1925 on the River Laxford and Loch Stack salmon fishing, with one of her largest catches on 30 September 1925, with a 17lb haul. Such was Chanel's legend for fishing, she recounted that she chanced upon a Scottish man at the Ritz,

Coco Chanel with Marcelle Meyer on the *Flying Cloud* in 1928, showcasing her yachting look.

Paris, who asked if she was the same Mademoiselle Chanel whose name was in the record books at Lochmore.[15]

'I learned to fish for salmon. For a year I watched, and I found it very dull,' she said. 'And then I tried it, and I fished from daybreak to eleven at night. I adored it. Obviously I was lucky; I fished only the best rivers. I even went to Norway, but up there I wasn't allowed to fish because the salmon were too tough. They'd bite off your fingers easily.'[16]

Winston Churchill visited the couple in Sutherland in September 1927, which was Chanel's third annual visit to Westminster's Scottish estate. Days were spent fishing on the river, and evenings in Stack Lodge involved playing bezique, a popular 1920s card game, by the roaring fire.

Churchill wrote to his wife Clementine in early October 1927 from Stack Lodge: 'Coco is here in place of Violet. She fishes from morn till night, & in 2 months has killed 50 salmon. She is (very) agreeable – really a (great) & strong being fit to rule a man or an Empire.'[17]

Misia also visited Chanel in Scotland at some point in the late 1920s. Chanel biographer Claude Delay recalled Chanel telling her that Misia 'felt like a fish out of water in Scotland. One day she wanted to go to the post. Coco told her it was twenty miles away and asked her if she could ride a horse.'[18]

As a commitment to Chanel, Westminster established a Highland escape, Rosehall House, giving her free rein to redecorate it in her own style. The house on Rosehall Estate,

The River Laxford, where Chanel spent the summer of 1925 salmon fishing with the Duke of Westminster.

located near Lairg, was sold by the Duke of Westminster in 1930, and left derelict from 1967. As it fell into disrepair the interiors disintegrated, yet Chanel's touches lingered on in the decaying walls with the beige colour scheme evident on the painted doors, skirting boards, and timber mantelpieces. Bedrooms were decorated with French floral blockprint wallpaper and a pale pink and beige flower design, while the remaining traces of beige pinstriped wallpaper in the downstairs twin reception rooms hinted at her panache.[19]

Chanel's bathrooms in Rosehall featured bidets, and while it has been claimed this was the earliest example in Scotland, the bidet was first manufactured by Shanks in Glasgow in the early 1900s, with Chanel's model from 1912. As well as exporting them to the French market, Shanks may well have supplied to other fashionable homes in Scotland.[20]

There was also a very large wine cellar at Rosehall, which would have been ideal for entertaining. 'This is a (very) agreeable house,' wrote Winston Churchill to his wife in May 1928.[21]

In the Highlands, Chanel developed her love for masculine clothing, and often borrowed the Duke's tweed coats when she was cold, as she had done with previous male companions. She posed with Vera Bate by the front door of Lochmore, dressed in men's sports clothing – Chanel in Westminster's tweed hunting jacket and flannel trousers, with the long sleeves and cuffs rolled up, sturdy boots, cardigan and cravat.

While Chanel's collections from 1923 had been marked with a Russian influence, her luxury sports clothes reflected her time with Westminster and the clothes she borrowed. *Vogue*, in 1926, reported that 'tweed is an essential of the smart new wardrobe'. Sourcing the tweed fabric for her luxurious cardigan-style tweed jackets, Chanel worked with Carlisle mill Linton Tweeds, founded by highly regarded Scottish textile producer William Linton. He used light boucle woollens in pastels and jewel tones, transforming traditionally rough tweed into a feminine fabric that was popular with the jazz-age denizens of the twenties.

Linton was born in 1872, in Selkirk, a Scottish Borders town that, from the eighteenth century, grew around cloth manufacturing, and where locals were guaranteed jobs in the mills, learning skills such as weaving, darning and dyeing. Linton began working as a

Above: At Rosehall House, traces of Chanel's rose-beige wallpaper are still evident under the more modern floral design.

Below: The Rosehall Estate near Lairg was Chanel and the Duke's Highland sanctuary in the late 1920s.

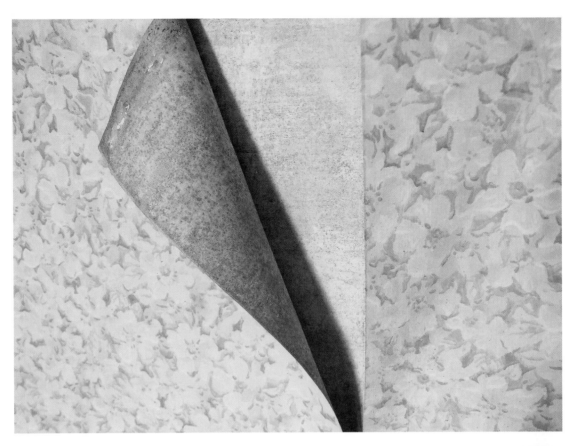

A 1929 *Vogue* illustration
depicting Chanel's sports
ensembles, which defined
her British look of that period.

tweed-maker in Hawick, before taking his business over the
border to Carlisle, where he established Linton Tweeds in 1912, as
a supplier for the luxury market. Chanel was introduced to Linton
in 1928 by fashion designer Edward Molyneux, who was also part
of her wealthy Monte Carlo set.[22]

Chanel's tweed cardigan jackets were worn with pleated skirts
and ropes of pearls, like the ones the Duke bestowed on her every
birthday. She brought French style to traditional, masculine hunting
clothing. She told Paul Morand: 'I brought in tweeds from Scotland;
home-spuns came to oust crepes and muslins. I arranged for
woollens to be washed less, so that they kept their softness; in
France we wash too much. I asked wholesalers for natural colours; I
wanted women to be guided by nature, to obey the mimicry of
animals. A green dress on a lawn is perfectly acceptable.'[23]

Chanel became one of the most prestigious designers to
champion Scottish textiles, utilising them in every collection – Fair
Isle tricot, tweeds, tartan and cashmere, the last still created in a
Scottish Borders mill, Barry's Knitwear, to this day. In 1933, Harvey
Nichols advertised a Chanel ready-to-wear sweater: 'You simply
must have at least one of these jumpers ... the latest creation of
Mademoiselle Chanel but actually made in Scotland.'[24]

During moments of urgency, when Chanel was anxious about
her collections, Westminster shipped her seamstresses to Eaton,
and it was here that the footman and butler uniforms of striped

waistcoats helped shape what became Chanel's 'British Look'. The Duke would be a supporting face in the audience for her twice-yearly shows, held every 5 February and 5 August.

In 1927, Westminster lent Gabrielle a Mayfair townhouse on Davies Street, close to his Queen Anne style mansion Bourdon House, and as well as staying there, she used the space for a boutique aimed at British society. With its prestigious address and Coco's fame, the boutique immediately attracted high-society names that included the Duchess of York, Daisy Fellowes, Lady Mary Davies, Diana Cooper and Diana Wyndham, the widow of Boy Capel.

The June 1927 edition of British *Vogue* announced: 'Chanel Opens Her London House'. Scheduled around the British society calendar, Chanel's collection featured white taffeta gowns for debutantes at court and afternoon dresses for Ascot in black lace and polka dots. The magazine praised her 'country tweeds' for sports and day dressing, with a 'white pique gardenia to the neck'. She understood perfectly the clothing required for the seasons, for Ascot, debutante balls and court introductions, for hunting season and the Glorious Twelfth.[25]

Chanel modelling her British Look suits in the gardens of her home at rue du Faubourg Saint-Honoré.

There was much speculation that Westminster and Chanel would tie the knot. The *New York Times* reported on 17 November 1928 that 'among recent guests at Eaton Hall, the residence of the Duke of Westminster, was the Paris dressmaker, Mme. Chanel. Her presence, according to the *News of the World*, has revived the rumors that Duke is contemplating a third marriage … since 1925 reports have been printed from time to time … that they would wed. He was reported to have spent $1,000,000 in refitting his yacht in 1925 in preparation for marriage with Mme. Chanel.'[26]

Chanel was less tolerant of Westminster's affairs and flirting with other women than she had been with Boy Capel, despite her reluctance to be pinned down with marriage. When Westminster brought a young, pretty woman on board the *Flying Cloud*, Chanel ordered he drop the woman at the next port of Villefranche. Dancer Serge Lifar wrote that: 'Proud and arrogant, Chanel couldn't stand being less than the one and only woman in Westminster's life. When the duke offered her the necklace, which was worth a fortune, Coco, in a gesture of superb defiance, let the pearls slide from her hand into the ocean.' In other accounts it was a huge emerald, and under the light of the full moon she leant against the rail and dropped it into the sea.[27]

Gabrielle was now in her forties, and aware that Westminster wanted an heir, she tried hard to fall pregnant but ultimately it was impossible. 'God knows I wanted love. But the moment I had to choose between the man I loved and my dresses, I chose the dresses. Work has always been a kind of drug for me, even if I sometimes wonder what Chanel would have been without the men in my life. Men don't understand that. They tell a woman, "I'll marry you. You can stop worrying, you won't have to work anymore." What they mean is, "you won't have to do anything except be there for me.'[28]

In spring 1930, the Duke married Bright Young Thing Loelia Ponsonby. Chanel accepted the end of the relationship, and declared she had been bored with the excessive, careless way of life. 'Fishing for salmon is not life. Any kind of poverty is better than that kind of wretchedness. The holidays were over. They had cost me a fortune, I had neglected my house, deserted my business, and showered gifts on hundreds of servants.'[29]

Previous page: Chanel enjoyed the beauty of Loch Stack while staying at the Duke of Westminster's sport's house, Stack Lodge.

Left: Chanel lambskin
coat and tweed dress,
modelled by Frances
Hope in *Vogue*, 1927.

Right: 'Westminster
Love', 2014, dry-point
etching, Charlotte Orr.

Coco was seated next to a diplomat, Sir Charles Mendl, at a dinner at the British Embassy in Paris, when he asked why she had turned down Westminster's proposal. She supposedly told him that there were 'so many duchesses already', and he replied: 'there's only one Coco Chanel'.[30]

In the London district of Mayfair, lampposts are embossed with gold interlocking 'C's' along with a 'W' for Westminster. Chanel romantics would have it that these symbols were placed there as a tribute from the Duke, to show she would always be in his regards. In reality the lampposts were positioned in the 1950s, with the interlocking 'C's' representing City Council and 'W' for the borough of Westminster, but they do share a strong similarity to Chanel's logo and offer a reminder of the British influence that helped shape her career.

Riviera Chic

'I remember from my childhood the immense staircase, with its steps worn from use. We used to call it the monks' staircase.'

Chanel on the staircase of the Great Hall, La Pausa. Photo by Roger Schall, 1938.

Roquebrune Cap-Martin
1929–1953

From its position looking out over the green, rocky coastline of the northernmost Côte D'Azur, with the glittering, moneyed Monte Carlo in the distance to the west, the Italian border to the east, and the foothills of the Alps as a backdrop, La Pausa was Coco Chanel's magnificent French Riviera sanctuary, located in Roquebrune Cap-Martin. With its painted shutters and terracotta roof tiles baking in the sun, it was an idyllic retreat that looked out towards the endless horizon. Chanel created the villa from the ground up, holding within its design the secrets of her childhood in Aubazine.

In Roquebrune the cicadas hummed from the olive trees, the smell of pine caught on the breeze and ancient paths meandered down the steep hills. This location was quite different from the coastal decadence so popular in the twenties. Rather than having a villa on the beach, Chanel preferred to enjoy the majestic, panoramic views of the deep-blue sea and mountainous coastline from high up. Stone steps led to the medieval village of Roquebrune, where its narrow streets had been built into the rocks and a castle watched over the headland. Chanel enjoyed striding up and down these paths. Her advice to stay fit was to 'walk in the open air on country roads with your head looking always forward – don't watch the earth as if you were glued to it'.[1]

For some visitors, La Pausa felt too isolated – the roads were difficult to navigate and Monte Carlo was a drive along hairpin bends and through rock-carved tunnels. But for Chanel, it offered solitude and the chance to live in simple luxury with the reminders of her past. The interior was completely different to her baroque apartment in Paris, which was filled with Coromandel screens, sculptures and ornate detail. In La Pausa, white and beige taffeta curtains complemented grey-tinted walls, and the floors were free from carpeting, with exposed terracotta tiles or parquet. In 1930, American *Vogue* called La Pausa 'one of the most enchanting villas that ever materialized on the shores of the Mediterranean … the house itself is long and Provençal, the grey of its walls melting into the soft tint of the wood of the olive trees'.

The Côte D'Azur had traditionally been thought too hot to visit in the summer. It was a fashionable winter destination for British and Russian aristocrats, with the villas and hotels closing up from May to October. By the 1920s, bohemian Americans drifted into the mix. Cole Porter recounted that he and wife Linda were considered crazy to rent the Château de la Garoupe in Antibes over summer 1921 and 1922. Gerard and Sara Murphy built Villa America, encouraging artists to visit for summer frivolity, and changed the attitude to the Riviera, where swimming in the sea, baking on rocks and enjoying picnics on the beach became the bohemian way of life for figures such as Pablo Picasso, Dorothy Parker and Jean Cocteau.

The jazz-loving, absinthe-drinking Lost Generation were also represented by F. Scott and Zelda Fitzgerald, who stayed at the Hôtel Belles Rives, situated on the beach at Juan-Les-Pins, and where Fitzgerald found inspiration beneath the palms for his acclaimed novel, *The Great Gatsby*. Chanel was even name-checked in *Tender is the Night*, with Nicole Diver wearing her scent: 'She put on the first ankle-length day dress that she had owned for many years and crossed herself reverently with Chanel Sixteen.'[2]

Coco Chanel, with her bronzed skin and love of sunbathing, helped the Riviera to become a year-round destination. She had already vitalised the popular beach resorts of Biarritz and Deauville with her wearable, practical sports clothes. She recounted that one day in the 1920s at the Lido in Venice, 'because I was growing tired of walking barefoot in the hot sand, and because my leather sandals were burning the soles of my feet, I had a shoemaker on the Zattere cut out a piece of cork in the shape of a shoe and fit two straps to it. Ten years later, the windows of Abercrombie in New York were full of shoes with cork soles.'[3]

Chanel celebrated Riviera style with her costumes for the 1924 collaborative ballet *Le Train Bleu*, by Diaghilev, which took its name from the exclusive sleeper train that transferred Paris society to the Riviera, making stops at Nice, Monte Carlo and Menton. The train, with its dark-blue carriages, evoked a sense of exotic escape, where you could find Charlie Chaplin, the Prince of Wales or Cecil Beaton resting in the sleeping cars as they were shuttled between London, Paris and the south of France.

Lydia Sokolova and Leon Woizikowsky in the Ballets Russes production of *Le Train Bleu*, November 1924.

The ballet depicted contemporary hedonism and social mores through familiar characters enjoying the sun, sea and sand, including a tennis champion based on Suzanne Lenglen and a golfer posed after the Prince of Wales. Ballets Russes dancer Lydia Sokolova wore Chanel's brilliant-pink knitted swimsuit with fake-pearl stud earrings and a bathing cap, setting a trend for what to wear on the beach. Cubist sculptor Henri Laurens designed the sets in neutral colours, with cubist waves, angular beach huts and parasols, and Picasso created the stage curtain. The French Riviera may also have inspired Chanel's double C logo. A similar design is emblazoned on windows in the Château de Crémat in Nice, once owned by Irène Bretz and designed in the early 1920s, and where Chanel is thought to have been a guest.

Chanel and the Duke of Westminster first visited the property destined to become La Pausa in 1927. At the time, it consisted of a main house and two smaller villas perched on the top of the promontory. Coco was drawn to the lush five acres of land with their olive groves and orange and mimosa trees, surrounded by meandering stone paths, and which, up until the nineteenth century, had been part of the Grimaldi hunting grounds. The name 'La Pausa', meaning 'to pause', was inspired by the myth that Mary Magdalene rested in the olive trees on her flight from Jerusalem, and Chanel hoped that the relaxed, idyllic setting could help her fall pregnant.[4]

It is often noted that the Duke paid the 1.8 million francs for the property, but it was Chanel's name only on the deeds of sale, signed at a Nice mortgage office on 9 February 1929.[5] Chanel was now incredibly wealthy in her own right, with boutiques in Cannes and Monte Carlo, and having bought many of the buildings on rue Cambon in Paris, she could have afforded this property herself.

Roquebrune had few houses in those days, but another avant-garde figurehead, Irish interior designer Eileen Gray built her own modernist home E1027 on its rocky shoreline in 1927. Gray, like Chanel, not only chose numbers to represent her ideas, but favoured contrasting black and white and designing functional pieces. While Chanel made clothes to enhance a woman's life, Gray created furniture for practical, easy living, including a steel tubular table that could be converted for breakfast in bed.

Eileen Gray's E1027 villa, on the Roquebrune Cap-Martin coastline.

Next page: The beach and hills of Roquebrune Cap-Martin, looking west to Monte Carlo.

Instead of adopting the modernist and innovative flat-roof design of E1027, Chanel had a vision for a traditional Provençal home, fusing details of her past with absolute comfort. She hired twenty-eight-year-old architect Robert Streitz to build to her exact specifications. He was invited onboard the *Flying Cloud* yacht for a drinks party to discuss the project, and after three days he had created a plan. Coco's vision harked back to her childhood in the stark orphanage at Aubazine convent. She envisioned the simplicity of a Romanesque monastery, where white stucco walls were set against hand-baked terracotta tiles on the roof, and there would be an imposing stone staircase in the entrance. As she told Streitz, 'I remember from my childhood the immense staircase, with its steps worn from use. We used to call it the monks' staircase. That's what I want.'[6]

Streitz visited Aubazine to see the staircase for himself, noting that the steps of the orphanage had been worn down over centuries of footsteps. It was in the hallowed cloisters of the abbey that inspiration was drawn for La Pausa's inner courtyard, with its archways and vaulted entrance.

Westminster insisted 'only the best materials be used', and the
builder Edgar Maggiore went to Italy to source the 20,000
handmade roof tiles to be used. Yet Chanel also wanted an aged
look, as if the house had been there for many years, and instructed
the carpenter to distress the shutters. 'Mademoiselle knew what
she wanted,' he told a reporter from *Galante*. Maggiore sent one
of his workers to Paris, so that Chanel could choose the exact
colour of the plaster to be used on the facade. Sometimes she
would hop on the *train bleu* to visit from Paris to see the progress
being made. Maggiore recalled: 'She was always in the best of
moods when she visited Roquebrune'. He added: 'On the site one
day she slipped into a pool of mud. Instead of lamenting the loss of
a dress, she laughed until the workers pulled her out.'

Eventually costing six million francs, more than three times the
purchase price, La Pausa was completed in 1929. The home had
three wings surrounding a monasterial courtyard, leading to the
dramatic Great Hall with its imposing staircase. It was here that

The cloisters of the Great
Hall at La Pausa, 1938.

Chanel incorporated the number five, her sacred number, throughout the house, with five windows above the entrance, a forged chandelier with five tiers, and a five-pointed star over her bed. The symbolism of five was evident in all aspects of Chanel's life, even at the Monte Carlo casino, with the *New York Times* reporting in 1926 that 'Chanel always plays the number 5'.[7] The fact that the home had five acres might even have been a factor in purchasing it.

As Chanel's modernist guests climbed the stone staircase or walked through the cloisters, it was unlikely they understood those memories and the reason behind her design choices. Chanel would rarely speak of her childhood, and when she did, she chose to tell the story of being raised by those two aunts, thin-lipped and dressed in black, rather than of the nuns in the convent. It was her own secret reinvention of her childhood home, and a celebration of her immense success in a code that linked her to her past.

Chanel in her bedroom in La Pausa, with five-pointed stars hanging above her bed.

The interior of the home was designed to be simple, cool and a reflection of the spartan quality of Aubazine. Edmonde Charles-Roux, the French *Vogue* editor and author of Chanel's biography, said: 'Whenever she began yearning for austerity, for the ultimate in cleanliness, for faces scrubbed with yellow soap; or waxed nostalgic for all things white, simple and clean, for linen piled high in cupboards, white-washed walls ... one had to understand she was speaking a secret code, and that every word she uttered meant only one word, Aubazine.'

Dark, heavy doors and sober furniture that included sturdy wardrobes in Chanel's bedroom and a cabinet at the bottom of the staircase, were reminiscent of pieces in the convent. She found luxury and comfort in austerity, just as she had embraced 'poverty chic' in her simple designs. 'Some people think luxury is the opposite of poverty. It is not. It is the opposite of vulgarity,' she said. Many of the sixteenth- and seventeenth-century pieces of furniture were Tudor or Jacobean, likely to have come from the Duke of Westminster's Eaton Hall. The remaining furniture was French or Spanish, having been selected by Chanel, even though items such as her Spanish wrought-iron chandeliers were considered unfashionable at the time.[8]

The greatest praise came from jeweller Fulco di Verdura, when looking around La Pausa, when he told her 'What genius to have spent all that money so that it doesn't show!' Coco believed that 'Nothing's more beautiful than emptiness. Furnish well, with peaceful things. Houses are like everything else, they have to have their souls made habitable. And a house ought to be natural. It ought to be like its owner.'[9]

In 1930, French *Vogue* published a spread on the completed house, showing the interiors in their simplicity, many rooms featuring bare parquet or tiled floors, unadorned with rugs and carpets. The dining room was shown to have a large rug under the table, a grand fireplace and double doors that opened out onto the garden, while the living area was decorated in beige, with fawn carpets imported from Spain and comfortable leather sofas to sink into. 'As soon as you lay down, bronze cushions went the colour of the books blending into the shelves,' said Coco. [10]

American *Vogue*'s editor Bettina Ballard recalled: 'It was beige, of course; even the piano was beige and all of the

Left: A haute-époque wardrobe from La Pausa, similar to the austere furniture of Aubazine. Dallas Museum of Art.

Right: Seventeenth-century carved chair, which was on display at La Pausa. Dallas Museum of Art.

bedrooms. I was told the Duke of Westminster had done his yacht in beige, which started her on beige decoration, but I think it more likely that she gave him the beige idea. Chanel, who always has a theory for everything, said that she went to the country to relax and not to be diverted by colourful, disturbing backgrounds, and she was right.'[11]

During its first fifteen years, Chanel transformed La Pausa, adding more eclecticism as the 1930s progressed. Colour photos in the French magazine *Plaisir de France*, in 1935, depicted a large blue-and-white rug and a huge sofa now placed in the austere Great Hall, and by 1935 the cloistered walkway had been enclosed with glass to create a separate space from the courtyard.

The right wing of the house served as living quarters for Coco and Westminster, and following their separation in 1930, it was reserved for Misia Sert. The Duke's room had a simple cast-iron bed, with no rug on the parquet floor, while Chanel's bedroom was separated from his by a bathroom. Her mantra that 'it is only possible to relax if one is not diverted by colourful backgrounds' was evident in her bedroom. The walls were lined with

Top: Sun-shaped clock, chosen by Chanel for decor at La Pausa. Dallas Museum of Art.

Below: The sun clock on the wall of the Great Hall at La Pausa, in 1935.

eighteenth-century English oak panels. Curtains and bedspreads were beige taffeta, and hanging above her Spanish, gilt, wrought-iron bed were five-pointed stars and amulets, for fertility. As in the rest of the home, a roaring fire kept the bedroom warm, as Coco rejected the idea of central heating. She liked mosquito nets to be draped over the bed and tucked in for protection.

If rue Cambon's aesthetics reflected the Orientalist and art deco trends of the 1920s, La Pausa and its ascetic white walls marked Chanel's preference for simplicity. The white-and-beige colour scheme was incredibly on-trend for the 1920s.

Eileen Gray's E1027 contrasted white with black and grey, using floor tiles in blocks of colour to create separate spaces in the open-plan living area and bedroom. Syrie Maugham was a champion of an all-white interior, and the Murphys' Villa America also developed a white-and-black colour scheme. Another major influence is thought to have been Eugenia Errázuriz's Biarritz house, La Mimoseraie, which attracted the avant-garde circle of Jean Cocteau, Pablo Picasso, Sergei Diaghilev and Igor Stravinsky. The Chilean-born society beauty, immortalised in a painting by John Singer Sargent, was proud of the 'very clean and very poor' look of her Biarritz home. She decreed that 'elegance means elimination', and was known for her explicitly svelte style. Eugenia favoured terracotta tiles and simple furniture, plain linen curtains and whitewashed walls, quite revolutionary for the belle époque era, and the utmost cleanliness where sheets and towels were scented with lavender. These touches were evident in La Pausa with its cool terracotta floor tiles and earthenware pots. The two women were also friends – when Eugenia became a tertiary Franciscan, Chanel designed a plain black habit for her.[12]

In the early 1930s, Chanel also chose white in her fashion designs, particularly for summer. 'A very white earring on the lobe of a well-tanned ear delights me,' she told Paul Morand, advocating her favoured beach look of bronzed skin against white.[13] White felt clean to Chanel – it had been the colour of the nuns' collars at Aubazine and of the freshly washed sheets and petticoats. In adulthood she chose plain, white, cotton sheets, as if from the convent. She said white 'mustn't look like whipped

cream', it had to dazzle. Of her spring 1933 collection, French *Vogue* wrote: 'A new way of presenting dresses adds to this powerful and palpable springtime feeling that reigns at rue Cambon. Chanel, for the first time, showed all her white dresses in one sitting. It was as if the place had suddenly been transformed into an orchard in Normandy.'

Chanel would wear whites on the tennis court at La Pausa, and at the Venice Lido in 1931 she was photographed in white beach pyjamas. By 1935, Chanel pyjamas were everywhere on the Riviera, and when asked what made her launch her beach pyjamas, she replied that it was a response to the unsightliness of people eating lunch at the Lido in wet swimsuits. Chanel particularly took to wearing trousers on the *Flying Cloud*, where it was tricky to climb up the ladder in a skirt. Such a casual use of slacks was really only available to the privileged few.

Chanel in white beach pyjamas and a sailor's cap at the Venice Lido, with Duke Laurino of Rome, 1937.

The *New York Times* reported in July 1931 that pyjamas 'seem firmly entrenched in fashionable circles … last Summer already saw them dining out in the casinos of Biarritz and Lido and this summer they are taken for granted in the smart resort wardrobe'. For evenings, Chanel created a popular 'white morocain gown with Turkish trousers with rhinestone anklets'.[14]

In La Pausa's gardens and courtyard, Chanel savoured the cool, dark cloisters and the tuberoses, lavender and irises climbing over the patio. If someone annoyed her, she would take lunch outside, eating alone under the olive tree. 'A tree grew inside the house. We lived underneath it,' she said. Chanel's gardener Marius Agneli ordered hundred-year-old olive trees to be taken from Antibes to be fixed in the garden. One olive tree

was planted in the middle of the pathway leading to the house, giving the impression that the path had been built around the ancient tree.[15]

The stucco walls formed a canvas for cactuses and cypress trees, while the olive trees were perfect for scrambling on. Luchino Visconti, a guest at La Pausa in the 1930s, and one of Rome's golden set, said Chanel was the first to cultivate 'poor' plants such as lavender, olive trees and cactuses, and to 'discard lilies, roses and flowers of that kind'.[16]

Étienne Balsan's brother, Jacques Balsan, and his wife Consuelo Vanderbilt, lived at Château Balsan at Èze. Winston Churchill would be a regular guest, enjoying painting in their garden – 'All shimmering sunshine and violet shades.'[17] These violet hues filled the gardens of La Pausa, with Chanel's vast fields of lavender, just like those in full bloom in the regions around Aubazine. They would also offer inspiration for gowns in the 1930s. The purple of the lavender and irises would be introduced into her collection of chiffon dresses and violet velvet suits. From 1932 she chose blue sequinned gowns, the colour of the Mediterranean, and a winter 1938 blue-grey Grecian-style sheath and scarf, inspired by the grey stucco of her walls.

The comfort of the many guests who came to stay was of utmost importance, with the house designed to offer them freedom, while protecting Chanel's privacy. The left wing of the house was divided into a series of two-bedroom suites, each with two bathrooms, joined by a private hallway, thus giving the guests – who tended to arrive in couples – complete discretion. Each bathroom had a servant's entrance so that the bath could be drawn and clothes taken away for cleaning and pressing without any disturbance. An electric call system alerted servants as to which room needed attendance. Bettina Ballard recalled 'The maid could discreetly enter the baths and dressing rooms through the foyer to give efficient, but unseen, service. Breakfast came when you rang, with the coffee and hot milk in thermos jugs so you could go back to sleep and awake to hot coffee again later. The house was blissfully silent in the morning.'[18]

Chanel's hosting was unusual at the time, and she fashioned a new, relaxed style of entertaining on the Riviera. Bettina added

In the lavender fields with
dog Gigot, La Pausa, 1930.

that: 'La Pausa was the most comfortable, relaxing place I have ever stayed.' It was a complete contrast to the English country life that Chanel had experienced on her visits with the Duke of Westminster. 'Everyone forever doing needlepoint, looking at rose gardens, changing their clothes, boiling in front of a fire and freezing away from it,' she would say. 'In her own home she wanted to be left alone unless she chose to be seen, and her guests had the same privilege,' Bettina added.[19]

Rather than set meals served sitting down, lunches and dinners were served buffet-style from a table by the window of the dining room. The large neo-Gothic oak table, probably salvaged from a school, was laid without a tablecloth, and guests would gather there informally with their filled plates.

They helped themselves to hot Italian pasta, English cold cuts, baked potatoes, caviar, fresh chestnut purée and classic French dishes, all washed down with chilled Riesling, Chianti or Beaujolais. Bettina continued: 'At lunch everyone moved around from the table to buffet trying new dishes, pouring big glasses of strong red wine, cracking nuts to eat with soft sweet dried figs. The meal would go on and on, often until four o'clock like a storytelling scene from Boccaccio.'[20]

With a rule of silence in the mornings, and with guests encouraged to take breakfast in their rooms, lunch was the first chance to be sociable. 'No one ever missed lunch – it was far too entertaining,' said Bettina. Chanel ate little, preferring to stand by the fireplace, her hands in her pockets as she prattled off anecdotes, dressed in black slacks, a slip-on sweater and ropes of pearls. To Visconti, La Pausa was 'a golden world', where Chanel's dinner parties were wonderfully entertaining, with no more than ten or twelve people.

While guests rarely ventured from Roquebrune, there were chauffeurs ready to drive guests down to the rocky beaches for a swim or to Monte Carlo to shop or to visit the casino. Sometimes they would drop in at other villas, such as Daisy Fellowes' Les Zoraides, which featured a swimming pool and huge manicured grounds. But most evenings were spent in conversation by the fire, sipping thimbles of vodka, or listening to Misia play piano. When Churchill came to visit, Coco played piquet with him, letting him win to keep him in an amiable mood.[21]

View from the back of
La Pausa, looking south
over the Roquebrune
Cap-Martin coastline.

Throughout the 1930s, Chanel spent most summers at La Pausa, and her home, filled with important, fascinating guests, served as a backdrop for major events of that era. As Claude Delay noted: 'When the house at Roquebrune smelt of tuberoses they used to say, "Mademoiselle is back".'[22]

It wasn't just Chanel who found La Pausa an inspiration for her work. Salvador Dalí and his wife Gala stayed at the villa from late summer 1938 until early 1939. Using the home for his surrealist visions, the artist created some of his major works in the house. There is a photograph of him reclining on the library mantel and another of him on the floor of the Great Hall displaying some of his significant works – *Palladio's Corridor of Dramatic Disguise*, *Debris of an Automobile Giving Birth to a Blind Horse Biting a Telephone* and *The Sublime Moment* among them. There were rumours that Dalí and Chanel had a brief affair, and in one letter from Dalí, written in late 1938, he called her a 'beautiful little bird' who has 'truly enchanted La Pausa'.[23]

Chanel sold La Pausa in 1953, to Hungarian publisher Emery Reves, who was also Winston Churchill's literary agent, and whose partner Wendy was a popular New York model. Chanel hosted a

dinner for Emery and Wendy to finalise the sale, saying, 'It is part of my past now and I don't wish to go back to it; its charm is something that you will discover for yourselves.'[24] The home needed a lot of work at the time, with the garden and tennis courts having long been neglected, and the interiors much as they were before the Second World War. The Reves transformed the home to suit their tastes, painting over the natural oak panelling, and adding modern furniture. They were avid art collectors and filled the home with Impressionist works by the likes of Manet, Monet and Renoir.[25]

While Coco's visitors included Igor Stravinsky, Pablo Picasso, Paul Iribe, Salvador Dalí and Luchino Visconti, the Reves's guests included Noël Coward, Greta Garbo, Errol Flynn, Clark Gable, Princess Grace of Monaco and Aristotle Onassis. The couple gave an entire floor to Winston Churchill, and it was in this cool Mediterranean home, with the spectre of Chanel's influence, that he wrote his memoirs.

Left: Blue sequinned evening gown, 1930s, reminiscent of the shimmering Mediterranean sea.

Right: The pale lace of this romantic evening gown, from 1936, resembles the colour of the flowers found in La Pausa.

Chanel in the 1930s

Chanel photographed in
her rue Cambon salon by
Boris Lipnitzki in 1937.

Paris
1930–1939

Chanel's affair with the 2nd Duke of Westminster came to an end in the spring of 1930, when the Duke married Loelia Ponsonby. In Paris, he took his wife to meet Chanel. Loelia recalled being shown into the 'luxurious and lavish' sitting room of Chanel's apartment on rue du Faubourg Saint-Honoré, where the fashion icon sat in a large armchair in front of a set of tall Coromandel screens. 'I perched, rather to a disadvantage, on a stool at her feet, feeling that I was being looked over to see whether I was a suitable bride for her old admirer – and I very much doubted whether I, or my tweed suit, passed the test,' wrote Loelia.[1]

Chanel's famous suppers for Sergei Diaghilev were sought-after events. To mark the end of the Ballets Russes' 1929 season, she held a party at her Faubourg Saint-Honoré home. Lanterns lit up the garden, a jazz band played and guests were served caviar and champagne. Serge Lifar, a close friend of Chanel's and a star of the Diaghilev ballet said: 'We drank torrents of champagne. As always, Coco began to turn on the men. She purred, and let everyone believe she could be seduced. Then, suddenly, she was gone. She disappeared at 2a.m., so she wouldn't miss her beauty sleep. She let men believe everything was possible, but didn't yield anything. That was her drama. She is looking for happiness, for love. She found it once: Boy Capel, a gorgeous Englishman who had everything, money and charm. So, instead, fame and success became her revenge.'[2]

Even after Diaghilev's death in Venice, in 1929, Chanel continued hosting lavish parties in her salon. Her niece, also Gabrielle, recalled these house parties in the 1930s: 'I remember an enormous house with a garden that went on forever, as far as the avenue Gabriel, and the stunning parties she threw there. I was just a little girl who had to go to bed early in the Faubourg era, as my aunt used to call it, but one of these events stands out in my memory even so, in honour of Diaghilev, with bands playing and laughter and the garden all lit up.'[3]

In July 1931, in the midst of a sweltering summer, Chanel held a garden party with guests that included Étienne Balsan's brother

Jacques and his wife, the Duchess of Alba, Gloria Swanson, Grand Duke Dmitri Pavlovich, and Baron Eugène de Rothschild and his wife. The *New York Times* wrote: 'She spread a huge tent made of gold tissue illuminated by hidden projectors, and at the end of this gold pavilion was a great floral screen of white hydrangeas, lilacs and lilies. Entertainment from dancers and orchestras of the Ambassadeurs across the street ... Chanel's parties are known for their superb decorations and profusion of artistic talent. The hostess was in white, matching the floral screen.'

Diana Vreeland, who described Chanel's features as 'just like a little bull, deep Dubonnet-red cheeks', was invited to Faubourg Saint-Honoré during this period. 'It had an enormous garden with fountains, the most beautiful salons opening on the garden,' she said. 'There she received the world. It was a proper society she had around her – artists, musicians, poets – and everyone was fascinated by her.' [4]

'I used to give two or three dances a year, and dinner parties,' recalled Chanel. 'Never a big formal table. Waiters to serve, but always a cold buffet. One can live without servants. I'd lived in England, hadn't I! The English breakfast – at Westminster's there was cold meat and porridge ready at any hour of the day or night. You need drink for the guests and for the music. They used to stay at my place till nine in the morning, and had to be told to go out through the garden, the way they'd come in.'

The carefree 1920s came to a sudden end with the Wall Street Crash of 1929, and as the wealthy lost vast amounts of money overnight, the bar bills ran dry in New York and Paris, and those who had bought gowns on credit couldn't pay the fashion houses. The situation affected many of Chanel's fellow designers, including Paul Poiret, who went into bankruptcy, and it made an overnight impact on style.

From the *la garçonne* look, so popular in the twenties, the fashion of the Depression years was one of seductive luxury – floor-skimming gowns in pale, tactile fabrics that clung to the body. Feminine glamour and real jewels offered a fantasy to escape from mass unemployment and foreclosures. In February 1930, Chanel created two floor-length evening gowns, one black and one white, and both demonstrating the dropped hem, raised waist and body-skimming shape of the next decade. [5]

Mrs William T. Wetmore wearing a long black satin and lace dress by Augusta Bernard; and Mrs Tilton Holmsen wearing a long tulip-print white organza dress by Chanel. *Vogue*, 1934.

For spring 1931, Chanel created popular crepe and organdie gowns in white, peach and coffee colours, incorporating whimsical tulle, velvet, lace and ribbon elements, reminiscent of the belle époque era before the war. She designed an organdie dress, 'for a girl that's poor, with a body. And if you add a turban and a piece of jewellery, she can go into a restaurant and everyone will say, isn't she pretty!' As French *Vogue* wrote in June 1930, of a Chanel ruffled organdie dress, 'There is nothing more worthy of the grace of a young girl than the simple organdie, freshest fabric among all, which is here treated in little ruffles.'[6]

Chanel embraced romantic innocence, yet she also continued to use tweeds and velvet, with jackets over stark white blouses with ruffled collars. 'Caterpillar during the day, butterfly in the evening,' she would say. A signature Chanel look was a black dress with contrasting white collars and cuffs, resembling a French maid's uniform, or a nun's habit, forged from the memories of the convent at Aubazine.

Despite Chanel's promotion of faux jewellery as an indicator of good taste, real gems came back in vogue in the 1930s, as part of this trend for luxurious glamour. To reflect this, Chanel created an exclusive collection of diamond jewellery 'Bijoux de

Left: Chanel in 1939, wearing a signature white ruff blouse and black jacket.

Right: The Bijoux de Diamants collection, 1932.

Diamants' that went on display at her Faubourg Saint-Honoré apartment in November 1932, with the jewellery exhibited against a backdrop of rich Coromandel screens. These diamond pieces were of cosmic design, inspired by the star and moon patterns of the monks' mosaic floor at Aubazine. There was a diamond bow-tie choker, a constellation that wrapped around the neck and a diamond fringe for hanging across the forehead. Conscious of maintaining value, many pieces were multipurpose – earrings that could be worn as brooches, necklaces that could also be tiaras. [7]

To protect her fashion house from the effects of the Depression, Chanel sought ways to cut costs, offering discounts on her clothes and jewellery and replacing silk with cotton for some of her gowns. She gained a boost from Hollywood, when Samuel Goldwyn offered her $1 million to design costumes for his film studio, having been introduced in Monte Carlo through Dmitri. Despite the Depression, American audiences were still going to the cinema in droves, desperate to see the latest movies with their favourite stars in show-stopping costumes, and Goldwyn believed Paris's leading couturière could help enhance his profits through her designs.

Coco and Misia sailed for New York on 25 February 1931, then travelled cross-country to Los Angeles by train, in a carriage decorated in white and stocked with champagne. Chanel was greeted at Union Station by a mob of reporters, and was invited to a whirl of parties to meet Hollywood's top tier: Marlene Dietrich, Claudette Colbert, George Cukor and Katharine Hepburn.

Samuel Goldwyn had promised Chanel a workroom and a staff of cutters, embroiderers and dyers at her disposal, and she set to work. Her first movie was *Palmy Days*, a chorus musical for which she designed costumes for star Barbara Weeks.

Chanel soon tired of her own palmy days and the 'vulgarity' of swimming-pool parties in Los Angeles, so Goldwyn agreed she could design her next film, *Tonight or Never*, in Paris, since its star, Gloria Swanson, was also in France, living it up with Noël Coward and her new husband Michael Farmer. Swanson visited rue Cambon for fittings, where Chanel fiercely demonstrated her displeasure that Swanson had gained weight and struggled to fit into a black bias-cut gown.

In fact, Swanson had fallen pregnant by Farmer and was due in four months. The actress wrote in her memoir of how Chanel berated her to lose weight. 'You have no right to fluctuate in the middle of fittings. Take off the girdle and lose five pounds. Five pounds. No Less!' Swanson tried to explain that for health reasons she couldn't lose the weight. Instead, a knee-length undergarment was created, into which she had to be hoisted, and which then held in her stomach while she was squeezed into the dress. When *Tonight or Never* was released, Chanel's elegant designs were deemed not showy enough for Hollywood tastes, fizzing rather than sparkling, and the film was not the success that had been expected.[8]

The third, and final, Goldwyn film Chanel designed for was *The Greeks Had a Word for Them*, a hit 1932 film about three rival gold-diggers. *Vogue* praised the white satin pyjamas designed for Ina Claire, much like the ones Chanel had worn on the Venice Lido, and which sparked a huge trend in the 1930s.

By 1931, Chanel had 2,400 staff working in twenty-six ateliers, and designed around 400 pieces for each of her shows on the 5 February and 5 August every year. As Janet Flanner noted: 'Chanel cannot sketch and doesn't like to sew. Apparently, she describes what she wants to a premiere, who then turns up with the rough form, which Chanel invariably finds all wrong.' She was uncompromising in the way she treated her staff and her customers, and with her low voice, her wide mouth, her eyes described as 'the color of sweet dates', she could let forth a flow of uncompromising words, and kill with one fiery look of disdain.[9]

Instead of making preliminary sketches, Chanel formed her designs by making a pattern from cottons, called a *toile*, and then pinning it together. She draped material over live mannequins, pricking them with pins while cutting and shaping the fabric, as she ordered them to stand straight for hours at a time until she was satisfied. 'Fashion is architecture,' she stated. 'It is a matter of proportions.' The premieres in the workroom would then use the *toile* to construct the final garment in its real material.

'Chanel terrified me on my first visit to the rue Cambon on *Vogue* business,' Bettina Ballard confessed, having been hired as the Paris fashion editor for the magazine in 1934. 'While she talked, her snapping black eyes holding me where I stood, I had

Gloria Swanson in a black Chanel evening gown in *Tonight or Never*, 1931.

time to look at her. She was small and built like a boy, her check-fronted vest sweater was hung with pearls, which I assumed were real, and she had a very special stance – hips forward, stomach in, shoulders relaxed, one foot forward, one hand plunged deep in her skirt pocket and the other gesticulating angrily.'[10]

Bettina recalled the tirade of words that fell from her mouth. Coco told her: 'I make fashions women can live in, breathe in, feel comfortable in, and look young in. You see this skirt? It doesn't cling to me in any place. I can move. I can even run quickly if I want to. Look at you, hobbling along in a tube. You are young, you can learn ...'

Chanel's favoured customers were those who ordered twenty or thirty pieces at a time, as 'the one-dress customer just takes up time and wastes money'. Chanel nicknamed a particular type of customer an 'angel' or 'darling'. Incredibly wealthy, the client tended to be called 'Dora, Daisy, Dorothea, Diane', she bought on credit and either returned a gown the day after a soirée or tried to barter it down to half price. Chanel wryly commented an 'angel never pays in cash ... an angel pays on the never-never'.[11]

The rue Cambon workrooms of Atelier Chanel, 1933.

With her vast wealth, enhanced by the success of Chanel N°.5, Chanel acquired the writer Colette's house at Montfort-l'Amaury, as well as a furnished flat in Venice, to add to her collection of properties. She also bought a moated Normandy château at Mesnil-Guillaume, near Lisieux, where she went boar hunting. French *Vogue*, in September 1931, described it as a fairy-tale castle, 'deliciously solitary', with its red and white towers and red-tiled roof reflected in the mirrored waters of its moat.[12]

The article described the 'majestic stone staircase' and a 'picturesque interior court with its wing of carved wooden posts', stained glass windows and steps with a 'delicate iron railing'. The large salon had blond wood panelling, natural wood chairs covered in lemon-yellow velvet, eclectic pieces of Louis XV furniture and sets of ceiling-height panelled windows. As with the stone steps she had created in La Pausa, Chanel was attracted to the grand stone staircase with balustrades leading up to a hallway with exposed wooden beams.[13]

The medieval style of this home may have inspired a range of gowns that were showcased in French *Vogue* in February 1931. It described 'A dress made of gold satin and not lamé … remarkable for its cross line and the importance of its sleeves', and also a pale-green mousseline dinner gown with very long

Drawing of the château at Mesnil-Guillaume, in Calvados, Normandy, which Chanel purchased in the early 1930s.

medieval sleeves, the waist nipped in with a rhinestone belt. Chanel admired the Florentine decorations of the Medicis, often covering dresses with Byzantine crosses.[14]

Following her relationship with the Duke of Westminster, in 1932, Chanel embarked on a love affair with Paul Iribe, an illustrator, costume designer and interior designer, born to Basque parents in Angouleme, southwestern France, in 1883. Iribe began his career drawing for satirical magazines at the age of seventeen, and his modernist illustrations were brought to the attention of Paul Poiret, who hired him to create drawings of his collections. These were published in 1908 in a book called *Les Robes de Paul Poiret*. Iribe's first wife, actress Jeanne Dirys, had worn a broad-rimmed Chanel hat in 1911 on the front cover of *Comoedia Illustré*. In 1919 Iribe moved to Hollywood where he created costumes for Cecil B. DeMille's epic movies. After a fall out with the director, Iribe returned to Paris with his wealthy second wife Maybelle Hogan.

With Maybelle's money, Iribe opened a shop on rue du Faubourg Saint-Honoré – not far from Chanel's apartment, where he sold his own furniture and jewellery designs. Iribe was one of a circle of drug-dependent artists that included Misia Sert and Jean Cocteau, and he was intense, fiercely patriotic and anti-Semitic.

Back in Paris, Iribe relaunched his political magazine *Le Temoin* in 1933, which he had previously run from 1906 to 1910, before moving on to different projects. This time partly funded by Chanel, *Le Temoin* featured Iribe's dark, nationalistic political illustrations, some of which used Chanel as a model for Marianne, France's symbol of liberty, making public their affair. The writer Colette called Iribe a 'most interesting demon' and, like her other friends, was appalled that Chanel was with him.

Describing their relationship as passionate, Iribe was one of the few people Chanel told the truth about her past. She recounted how she and Iribe set out 'on the trail of my youth' and visited Moulins and the convent at Aubazine. 'We found the house of my aunts,' she said. 'As I walked beneath this avenue of lime trees, I really felt as if I were beginning my life again.'[15]

Theirs was an intense relationship, with Chanel lamenting: 'The most complicated man I ever knew was Paul Iribe. He criticised

A Chanel necklace of gilt bronze with paste, glass and imitation pearls, National Museums Scotland.

Above: Gown, worn with matching cape, of camellia-patterned lace over pale fawn silk crepe, early 1930s, National Museums Scotland.

Below: Pale pink-grey silk gauze evening gown, with draped back, circa 1930, National Museums Scotland.

me for not being simple.' He chastised her for living in such a
large townhouse at Faubourg Saint-Honoré, asking her why she
needed all her servants and her furnishings.[16]

To appease him, she gave up her grand apartment, and
instead rented two rooms in a small house near rue Cambon.
'Since this modest accommodation did not include any
bathrooms, I had one built,' she said. 'I installed another,
arranged my favourite books, a Coromandel screen, two heaters
and a few fine rugs.' She told him she was now 'boarding out'
and 'living the famous simple life'. Yet he was annoyed that she
really had moved out of her opulent home.

'You wanted me to leave the wood panelling, the marble and
the wrought iron: here's my cottage. The concierge does her
cooking on the stairs. Your feet knock into empty milk bottles,' she
recounted that she told him. 'Isn't this the life you wanted me to
lead and that you yourself want to lead?'[17]

Declaring that he wasn't used to living in 'such hovels', they both decided to move into the Ritz, and her furniture, objects and clothes were moved into the third floor of 31 rue Cambon. She considered her real home to be La Pausa, with her life in Paris now based at the Ritz or at her boutique. Sacrificed in this move was her butler Joseph, whom she ruthlessly dismissed after sixteen years' loyal service. This dramatic move also sought to cut costs because of the Great Depression.

In September 1935, Iribe travelled from Paris to visit Chanel at La Pausa, and on the morning of his arrival, he joined Chanel for a match on the tennis court. Halfway through the game she came up to the net to chastise him for hitting the ball so hard. He looked over his sunglasses, stumbled and collapsed to the ground from a massive heart attack. He was whisked to a clinic in Menton, but passed away without gaining consciousness. To see him die in front of her was a trauma that stayed with Chanel, and she never used the tennis court again, neglecting it until it was reclaimed by grass and weeds. Heartbroken once more, she threw herself back into work to help bring her peace.

Returning to Paris from La Pausa to prepare for her 1936 collections, Chanel chose to remain classic, with peplum tunics and tweeds worn with skirts, but for the first time in her career, Chanel felt threatened by a new designer. Elsa Schiaparelli had become hugely sought-after for her surrealist, daring designs – fish-shaped buttons, lobster motifs from a collaboration with Dalí, and trompe l'oeil sweaters that made Chanel seem almost old-fashioned. Chanel rejected Schiaparelli's fashion, always referring to her as 'that Italian woman', and stating she preferred to choose style over fads, but fashion editors embraced the fun and colourful innovation of a Schiaparelli show.

Elsa Schiaparelli's apartment in the boulevard Saint-Germain was furnished with an orange leather sofa, stiff white rubber curtains and chair covers, and tables topped with black glass. When she held her first dinner party, she invited Chanel. 'At the sight of this modern furniture and black plates she shuddered as if she were passing a cemetery,' recalled Schiaparelli.[18]

Chanel devotees still adored the cut of her clothes and how they made them feel. Diana Vreeland said: 'I loved my clothes from Chanel. Everyone thinks of suits when they think of Chanel.

That came later. If you could have seen my clothes from Chanel in the thirties – the *dégagé* gypsy skirts, the divine brocades, the little boleros, the roses in the hair, the pailettes nose veils – day and evening. And the ribbons were so pretty.'[19]

Alongside her fashion line, Chanel was commissioned to design for film and theatre. Jean Renoir asked her to design costumes for his film *La Règle du Jeu*, set on a French country estate where life was similar to that of prewar Royallieu, with its fancy-dress parties and stag hunts, yet with an underlying theme of death. Chanel also created costumes for two Cocteau works – *Les Chevaliers de la Table ronde* and *Oedipus Rex*.

In 1936, a left-wing coalition was elected into power, and workers felt bolstered to go on strike to make demands for their rights. In June of that year, Chanel came out of the Ritz's rear entrance on rue Cambon, and was shocked to find her sales girls protesting outside, with photographers capturing the moment. 'It was cheerful and delightful. The accordion could be heard playing all over the house,' she later recalled. But in truth she took the strike as a personal affront and was angered by her staff. She felt they were ungrateful, particularly as she had bought the retreat at Mimizan to give her workers all-expenses-paid holidays for one week a year.

Despite the generosity to her friends, paying for Cocteau's continued detoxification cures and hotel bills, providing support to Stravinsky and Reverdy and funding Diaghilev, Chanel refused to give her workers a pay rise, regardless of the hours they put in. Chanel would say: 'They are gorgeous girls, why don't they find lovers. They should have no trouble finding rich men to support them.'[20]

The women on strike came to see her at the Ritz, but she refused them – she would do this on her terms. But when she arrived at her salon, dressed in ropes of pearls, her employees denied her access. As the strike went on, Chanel had to give in to demands in order to complete her autumn collection. When they eventually came to an agreement, Chanel fired 300 women who refused to sign it. 'What idiots those girls were', she declared.

Unrest was simmering across Europe in the late 1930s, Schiaparelli was grabbing the headlines in the fashion press, but

Chanel continued producing beautifully cut designs, despite losing some of her caché. In July 1938, British *Vogue* noted the romance of Paris evening fashions – 'hair is brushed into the clouds and sprinkled with jewels. Shoulders are bare, as in Chanel's famous black lace dress.' [21] Chanel, as Bettina Ballard recalled, had showcased to her a strapless, beautifully cut lace dress. 'At a time when evening dresses were strapped or V-necked, she had completely bared the shoulders and freed the figure, starting a whole new evening trend.'[22]

Chanel launched her gypsy collection in 1938, featuring puff-sleeved peasant blouses and embroidery, boleros, flamenco-style skirts and camellia flowers pinned to shoulders, and it was praised for its sex appeal and its colour – lightening the mood under the threat of war.

During the last months of peace in Europe, Chanel attended a whirlwind of parties and masked balls with themes that included the Oriental Ball, the Forest Ball and the Masterpiece Ball. At the Comte de Beaumont's Ball she dressed as La Belle Sans Merci, while Lady Mendl held a party for 700 at Versailles,

Left: Chanel's employees on strike outside the rue Cambon boutique in June 1936.

Right: A Chanel suit, from the February 1936 collection.

'If you could have seen my clothes from Chanel in the thirties – the dégagé gypsy skirts, the divine brocades, the little boleros, the roses in the hair...'

acting as ringmaster to ponies, clowns and acrobats. Gabrielle's escort that night was Arthur Capel's old friend the Duc de Gramont, and she spent much of the evening chatting with Wallis Simpson. The rest of the summer was spent at La Pausa.[23]

In September 1939, as war broke out, *Vogue* featured a photograph of Chanel in a tweed jacket, smoking a cigarette as she watches over a model in a velvet suit nipped in at the waist, with lace ruff collar and cuffs. 'Chanel's eye rests approvingly on the pinched waist of her velvet Watteau suit,' described the magazine. She was pictured as the grande dame keeping a watchful eye on her placing in the world.[24]

Chanel was at the Ritz when France declared war on 2 September, and three weeks later she closed down her fashion house and her almost 4,000 workers were let go, perhaps as punishment for their strikes. She kept 31 rue Cambon open, but would only sell her perfumes and jewellery, despite the French government asking her to continue designing in order to boost morale. Her last design before the war was a patriotic evening dress in the red, white and blue of the tricolor. It was a sudden end to more than two decades as a fashion leader, and it would be fifteen years before Chanel would sell another gown.

The autumn 1938 collection featured colourful, gypsy-inspired designs, as featured in *Marie Claire*, 23 September 1938.

At the Ritz

'I'm like a snail, I carry my house about with me. Two Chinese screens and books everywhere. I've never been able to live in a house that's left wide open – the first thing I always look for is screens.'

Paris
1935–1971

Chanel moved into the Hôtel Ritz permanently in July 1935, and the hotel became her Paris sleeping quarters for the rest of her life. She chose to live in a hotel because 'You can eat what you like, you needn't go out if you don't want to. Slavery, having to rush to lunch at a regular hour.'[1]

When it opened in 1898, the Hôtel Ritz was the home and meeting place of bohemian artists and intellectuals, stage actresses and courtesans. Situated at 15 Place Vendôme, it was formerly the site of the palace of the dukes of Vendôme and was situated next to the French Ministry of Justice.[2]

In the heart of the fashion district, surrounded by art nouveau teahouses, milliners and designers, the hotel stood for all things modern and extravagant. F. Scott Fitzgerald dreamed of diamonds as big as the Ritz, Irving Berlin wrote the song 'Puttin' on the Ritz' from the youthful Harlem expression for 'spending ev'ry dime for a wonderful time', and Ernest Hemingway once said: 'When in Paris, the only reason not to stay at the Ritz is if you can't afford it.'

Swiss founder César Ritz planned the layout of the hotel personally, with discretion and comfort in mind. There was no proper lobby so as to discourage lurkers and voyeurs, while the grand staircase was ideal for a dramatic entrance before dinner. It was Marie-Louise Ritz, after the death of husband César, who connected the eighteenth-century palace with two rue Cambon buildings via a long corridor, which was ideally suited to Coco Chanel's needs.[3]

Chanel made the journey every day from the Ritz's rue Cambon entrance to her salon across the street. A hotel doorman would alert staff that she was on her way, so they could spray Chanel N°.5 to greet her. This also allowed her to avoid having to see Elsa Schiaparelli's glitzy boutique on Place Vendôme, which had opened in 1935. Schiaparelli referred to rue Cambon as the 'backside' of the Ritz. 'Poor Chanel, I use the front door of the Ritz, she must use the back.'[4]

The hotel's soft apricot lighting and its marble, wooden and gold design followed Chanel's favoured aesthetics. When she

Chanel in her suite at the Hôtel Ritz, Paris, 1937. Photographed by Francois Kollar.

moved into the Ritz in 1935, she was given a large salon on the third floor with elegant wood panelling and views onto Place Vendôme. Chanel's Ritz apartment was similar in design to her rue Cambon apartment, with honey hues and eastern-inspired features. 'I'm like a snail, I carry my house about with me. Two Chinese screens and books everywhere. I've never been able to live in a house that's left wide open – the first thing I always look for is screens.'

The living area was filled with her favoured Coromandel screens, beige sofas and gilded woodcarving, and was heated with a wood-burning stove. Her bedroom was deceptively simple. At her dressing table she had two vermeil boxes that had been given to her by the 2nd Duke of Westminster, her brushes and scissors, a chamois cloth with her jewellery and, on the wall, a pinned photo of her niece Gabrielle.

Bettina Ballard described her visit to see Chanel at the Ritz in the 1930s. 'Bébé Bérard, the artist, and I went to the Ritz late one afternoon to sketch the new way that Coco Chanel was wearing her sweaters: plastered with pearls and emeralds, worn with an easy jersey skirt, and wrapped twice around the waist with a grosgrain ribbon that tied in a bow in front ... Chanel always has a fire burning. Her bones are always cold. She took me into her bedroom, which was a complete surprise; it looked like a small, antiseptic hospital room with a narrow bed with a rosary on the brass bedstead and a crucifix over the bed. There was a table and a straight chair – little else . . '[5]

Winston Churchill was a regular visitor to Paris in the late 1930s. He always called on Chanel, and there was one particularly memorable visit in December 1936. Jean Cocteau described in his diaries, a dinner in Chanel's suite with Churchill and his son, Randolph, at the time when Winston was in Paris to plead with Edward VIII not to marry Wallis Simpson. Cocteau recalled that Winston was very drunk when he cried on Chanel's shoulder, despairing that he was helpless to stop the King from abdicating.

The hotel was a sanctuary of privilege and wealth, and when war broke out in 1939 it offered a protective space for its glamorous guests. Many of Paris's wealthy residents closed their villas and moved into the perceived safety of the hotel after losing staff to the draft. Chanel paid for a 'rabbit hole' room for

Above: The dining room at the Hôtel Ritz in 2016. Chanel kept a table during her residency.

Below: The comfortable rooms at the Ritz were enjoyed by Chanel for five decades.

Cocteau; Reginald and Daisy Fellowes moved into the Royal Suite
and Lady Mendl took the Imperial Suite.

Chanel regularly dined with Cocteau and his partner Jean
Marais, actor Sacha Guitry and ballet dancer Serge Lifar, where
they could enjoy salade Niçoise, chilled Beaujolais, medallions of
veal, baked apple tart, followed by a cigarette and a cocktail at
the Bar Ritz.[6]

The Ritz had been a favourite retreat and playground for the
Duke and Duchess of Windsor throughout the 1930s. They spent
their honeymoon and enjoyed dinners with the dressmaker.

Chanel in her Ritz suite,
1937, wearing a navy-style
cap, inspired by her time
on the *Flying Cloud*.

Edward and Wallis even held a black-tie dinner in those first months of the war, interrupted briefly for an air raid. The cellars of the hotel were fashioned as air-raid shelters, complete with fur rugs and silk Hermès sleeping bags. Noël Coward, stationed in Paris as a member of the British war propaganda bureau, recalled seeing Coco Chanel on the way to the air-raid shelter, followed by a servant carrying her gas mask on a satin pillow.[7]

The staff at the Ritz shrank from 450 to twenty during the war. Chanel's two chambermaids and her chauffeur abandoned her, and she desperately sought another driver. She used morphine to sleep at night as war crept closer. From the windows overlooking Place Vendôme she saw 'clouds of black smoke darkening the sky – at three in the afternoon it was like nightfall as bits of charred paper covered the city's streets'.

The Germans were advancing on Paris, and Chanel decided that, for her safety, it was time to leave. She packed her belongings into huge trunks that were stored by the concierge, paid her bills for two months and found a new driver to take her out of the city, along with a couple of her faithful employees, joining the exodus on the roads choked with buses, trucks and cars.

La Pausa was too close to the Italian border for comfort: now that Mussolini had declared war on the Allies, bombs were falling on the Riviera. Instead, Chanel made the long journey to Pau, in the Pyrenees, where she had first met Boy. Her nephew André was living in the château in the village of Corbère – Chanel had bought it for him in 1926 – and her old friend Étienne Balsan was living in retirement there, too.

Her nephew's daughter Gabrielle remembered: 'Auntie Coco had somehow managed to send on her entire gold dressing table set which had been given to her by my godfather, the Duke of Westminster, and that came to our house separately.'[8] When Chanel arrived at the Château de Corbère-Abères she discovered that André, who had signed up to the French army, was now being held in a prisoner of war camp and his whereabouts and health were unknown.

There was plenty of food and homemade wine at the château, but hiding in the mountains proved to be too quiet. When it was clear the Germans wouldn't bomb Paris, she made the return journey with her friend Marie-Louise Bousquet. They stopped over in Vichy, and Chanel was struck by the celebratory atmosphere in the Hôtel du Parc, where the champagne flowed. All the hotels were overcrowded, but she managed to persuade the hotelier to let her sleep in a hot and stuffy garret room while her friend was given a chaise-longue in a linen room. The next day they sourced petrol, and after ducking roadblocks, they made the slow return to Paris on clogged backroads.

Chanel arrived back in Paris to find swarms of German soldiers around the place de la Concorde and standing guard at the Ritz's Place Vendôme entrance, now sandbagged and with a swastika flying above. When she asked for her old room, Chanel was told by a manager she must see the German commander who was now in charge. Chanel insisted she couldn't allow him to see her dirty and unwashed, so she instructed the manager to 'say that Mademoiselle Chanel has arrived. I'll go when I'm clean. I've always been taught that it's better to be clean when one is asking for something.'[9]

While the Place Vendôme side of the hotel was reserved exclusively for Germans officers, the rue Cambon side was for civilians. A small room on the top floor of that wing was found for Chanel, and she paid the Ritz to build a short flight of stairs from her two-room suite to a modest little garret bedroom.

The Ritz was neutral during the war. High-ranking German officers lived in opulence alongside American writers and wealthy French, some of whom were in the French resistance and others who were German collaborators. Because of this unique situation, the cocktail bar became a gathering place for the resistance, and Frank Meier, the legendary bartender at the bar on the rue Cambon side of the hotel, mixed cocktails while passing covert messages. The staff used the kitchens for resistance smuggling, while refugees hid in the eaves of the building.[10]

At Sunday evening dinner dances at the Ritz, glamorous Parisians mixed with German officers, encouraging affairs and romances that crossed diplomatic lines. French film star Arletty lived at the Ritz with her German lover, Hans-Jürgen Soehring, and she wasn't the only one. Chanel began an affair with a tall, blonde German officer, Hans Günther, Baron von Dincklage. He was thirteen years younger than Chanel, his nickname was

Coco Chanel with Baron von Dincklage in Villars, Switzerland in 1951. The photograph featured in *Paris Match*.

Spatz, meaning 'sparrow', and he had an English mother, as Chanel frequently protested when under fire for collaborating with the enemy. She told Cecil Beaton, 'Really sir, a woman of my age cannot be expected to look at his passport if she has a chance of a lover.'

Chanel was discreet, keeping her rue Cambon apartment for entertaining Spatz and her circle of friends, with dinner served beside the Coromandel screens. Chanel and von Dincklage often sneaked back into the Ritz through the rue Cambon entrance, where she had privacy in her third-floor rooms. Fern Bedaux, married to Nazi agent Charles Bedaux, stayed on the same floor of the Ritz as Chanel and reported that Chanel was addicted to morphine and 'every evening received Dincklage in her rooms'.[11]

Chanel, with Dincklage's authority, was free to travel between the occupied zones, and so she and Spatz travelled to La Pausa together on several occasions. The villa's architect Robert Streitz, now part of the French resistance, contacted Chanel and asked for help for a friend arrested by the Gestapo. Chanel was possibly unaware her huge wine cellars were being used as a secret space to send messages by transmitter, and that French Jews took refuge in La Pausa's gardens before escaping to the Italian border.[12]

Chanel also accompanied Spatz to Berlin in the winter of 1943. She was worried for her beloved nephew who was in an internment camp. It is also believed that she was asked by German intelligence to travel to neutral Madrid and to contact Winston Churchill and the Duke of Westminster in order for the Germans to broker an arrangement with the Allies.[13]

On 6 June 1944, the Allies landed in Normandy as part of D Day, and the Luftwaffe officers at the Ritz loaded up bounty from the hotel as they prepared to depart for the German frontier. Ernest Hemingway was determined to be the first American reporter to liberate Paris, and he swept into the Hôtel Ritz in the last hours of the occupation, freeing many bottles of vintage

American soldiers playing outside Chanel's boutique in 1945, after the liberation of Paris.

wine from its cellars. Von Dincklage tried to persuade Chanel to retreat with him, but she chose to stay in Paris, left alone with the collaborators and the resistance workers.

Chanel's relationship with von Dincklage raised questions, and in August 1944 she was taken for interrogation by les Forces françaises de l'intérieur. Punishment for women who collaborated was harsh and humiliating – their heads shaved, swastikas branded on their foreheads, imprisonment and even execution. Chanel was released after a couple of hours, after what was likely to have been an intervention from Winston Churchill. Arletty, however, was not so well protected: she was arrested in September 1944, found guilty of treason and sentenced to eighteen months' imprisonment. In response to Serge Lifar's collaboration, the Paris Opéra committee suspended him for a year. It was a light punishment in the face of feelings of anger and betrayal in liberated Paris.

There was a rumour that Chanel, as a measure to protect herself in American-liberated Paris, placed an announcement in the window of her boutique that bottles of Chanel N°.5 would be free for American troops for sending home as gifts to loved ones. Journalist Malcolm Muggeridge noted how astonishing it was that she got away with collaborating, but by offering free perfume to GIs, they 'would have been outraged if the French police had touched a hair of her head'.

When Muggeridge interviewed Chanel in September 1944, asking her which side she had been on, she replied: 'On neither side, of course. I stood up for myself as I always have done. Nobody has ever told Coco Chanel what to think.'[14]

To escape from any further interrogation, Chanel made for Switzerland, leaving her business, which had been the most important thing in her life. She reunited with Hans von Dincklage in Lausanne and they lived together in exile at the luxury Hôtel Beau Rivage on the shores of Lake Geneva, occasionally being photographed on the slopes at St Moritz. But in France, Chanel's role as 'horizontal collaborator' lingered bitterly, and her boutique lay empty. Von Dincklage left Chanel to move to the Balearic Islands, living the rest of his days in comfort on a pension provided by her. It's unknown whether the two met again.

After the war, when Chanel returned to Paris for her fashion comeback, she continued to live in the eaves of the Ritz, in her small wartime rooms, 304 and 305, which offered rooftop views to the Jardin des Tuileries and the Seine. 'I could have had the best apartment in the Ritz, but I preferred to live in a Garret. My three attics – one to sleep in, one to talk in, and one to wash in,' she said. She furnished her living room with Coromandel screens, wheat-beige sofas and velvet pin cushions pierced with hatpins.[15] After her death, the Ritz hung an artwork in her suite, which was discovered to be Le Sacrifice de Polyxène, by seventeenth century painter Charles Le Brun.

The bedroom was as stark as the rooms of a convent, with tall windows set into the slanting roof. Silk lampshades created a peachy glow against the pure white of the walls and sheets on her bed. Ears of wheat rested on the mirror, rows of scissors were laid out on a white cloth on the dressing table and a Russian Virgin hung over the bedrail of her brass bed. There were various treasures on her night table: a Byzantine cross, the replica of the tomb of St Anthony of Padua, and Boy Capel's black watch. It was a dressmaker's retreat, and it felt safe and comforting.

As her niece Gabrielle recalled: 'Every night, Coco would retire to the Ritz to sleep: there she felt secure, in a bedroom sandwiched by others, surrounded by life. After the war, she tried to sleep at rue Cambon, turning the third room into a bedroom. She had a rather bizarre bed made for it in sections of Coromandel screen, very low and imposing. She really did try to sleep there, but she admitted to me "I can't do it, I'm too frightened".'[16]

Chanel was well known around the Ritz, with guests often keeping an eye out for the figure in the straw boater hat, sitting at her usual table in the dining room. She was protected by the owner, Charles Ritz, and she also enjoyed the hotel life because all her whims were catered to. At Christmas 1963, the Ritz placed a high Christmas tree in the lobby of its rue Cambon entrance, stripping the tree of its needles and covering it in snow-white ostrich feathers, tinsel and gold baubles. 'You know that Mademoiselle Chanel lives here,' Charles Ritz said. 'She is such a nice woman and old friend. We did it as a surprise for her, because each year she complained about our dreary old trees.'[18]

Left: Chanel's suite at the Ritz before the Second World War offered views to place Vendôme, one source of inspiration for the shape of the Chanel N°.5 bottle.

Above: Chanel on the balcony of her suite at the Ritz in 1937.

10

The Comeback

'I enjoyed life at my country place in Switzerland. But I was bored not having anything real to do. Always, I observed the new clothes.'

Paris
1953–1971

Since 1939, the upper floors of Gabrielle's rue Cambon boutique had been deserted. The ground-floor shop had sold perfume throughout the war, but in the workrooms, the dress dummies were bare, and without the whir of the sewing machines, the atmosphere was hauntingly silent.

To escape the accusations of wartime collaboration, Chanel chose to base herself in Switzerland, not only to be able to spend time with Hans von Dincklage, but to avoid paying tax on her sizeable income. She was recorded as having stayed at the Hôtel Beau Rivage for long periods of time from 1945 to 1954, altering her date of birth to 1893 when registering, making herself ten years younger.[1]

She would travel to and from Paris, often with Misia, when the two would buy morphine from a pharmacy in Lausanne. Misia, once the muse of the greatest artists, was an eccentric with a drug addiction, Chanel was still lean and chic, but her wit had been replaced by cynicism. Chanel spent her days in Switzerland shopping, meeting with friends for conversation at the hotel, or over dinners in the historic streets of Lausanne, living on vegetable soup and filet mignon.

Chanel's third-floor rue Cambon apartment remained frozen in time, yet she still entertained there on visits from Switzerland, her image reflected in the endless mirrors of her staircase and salon as she trailed between her apartment and the Ritz.

It was at one of these gatherings that flame-haired model Suzy Parker persuaded Chanel to make a comeback. Suzy worshipped Chanel, dressing like her and adopting her stance. She had been invited to a card party at rue Cambon with *Elle* magazine's editor Hélène Lazareff. Chanel encouraged Suzy to rummage through the racks of clothes for something to wear for dinner. She selected a Chanel gown from 1938 and, seeing her so excited about it, Lazareff decided she wanted Suzy in Chanel on the cover of *Elle*.[2]

The Paris fashion scene had changed after the war. Madeleine Vionnet closed in 1939, Jeanne Lanvin died in 1946;

Suzy Parker in a Chanel suit, outside the French *Vogue* offices, 1954.

and by 1954 Schiaparelli had shut her fashion house. Instead, it was a designer named Christian Dior who represented Paris's postwar recovery. Dior created his 'New Look', named 'La Ligne Corolle', after the petals of a flower, using swathes of fabric for full skirts nipped in tightly at the waist. It was very feminine and excessive and it was an instant success.

Chanel had always challenged her rivals, and in reaction to Dior's excessive new look, she eyed a long-awaited return to fashion. 'Never was I really in retirement in my heart,' she told the *New Yorker* in 1957. 'During the war, nobody thought any more of making beautiful clothes, and after the war I watched the couturiers, the young men, to see what they were doing. I travelled. I enjoyed life at my country place in Switzerland. But I was bored not having anything real to do. Always, I observed the new clothes.'[3]

By 1953, Chanel's inner circle had diminished, and she had just a few close friends left. Misia Sert died in 1950, five years after José-Maria Sert, while Étienne Balsan was killed when struck by a car in Rio de Janeiro. When the 2nd Duke of Westminster died, in July 1953, Chanel realised it was time to let go of her past and put La Pausa up for sale. She also needed to raise money in order to fund her comeback.

The dressmaker returned to Paris, where she stayed at the Ritz, and in order to find further capital she began the process of selling off her buildings on rue Cambon – all except for number 31. The Wertheimers, owners of her perfume company, helped with finances, underwriting her business and gaining the rights to her name. They paid all her personal expenses and granted her creative control.[4]

In January 1954, Chanel set to work reopening 31 rue Cambon. The building consisted of the ground-floor boutique, the grand salon for showing the collections, her apartment on the third floor and her workrooms above that. She refurbished the building, and spent her days working from a small room with the help of an elderly fitter and one model on whom she could shape her designs. Rosamond Bernier of British *Vogue* reported in February 1954 of a visit to rue Cambon, 'until recently empty, dormant. We went through the boutique with perfumes, soaps, sweaters and scarves, into the mirrored hall of a mirrored

Carl Erickson sketch of Coco Chanel in her rue Cambon living room being interviewed by Rosamond Bernier. *Vogue*, February 1954.

staircase, strips of mirror breaking space into a colourless cubist maze beyond time and space, hushed with carpets. Past massive dull gold Spanish arabesques, past the darkened show-room sliced with lacquered screens, up the famous staircase where Chanel's openings had crowded her high-titled employees and the most brilliant personalities of the day.'[5]

Rosamond and her photographer were led through an entrance hall 'dark with panelled Oriental screens, pushing through the looking glass (more mirrored doors) into a small, dim study to find – not Sleeping Beauty – but a small, brown idol hung with jewels, perched on the edge of an outsized brown sofa … her extraordinary hands, monumental on a small scale: powerful, broad-knuckled, the hands of a sculptor, strong long fingers, short unpolished nails, massive emerald ring'.[6]

The date for Chanel's first collection in fifteen years was set for 5 February 1954, and fashion editors, photographers, buyers and high Paris society received highly sought-after invitations. The night before the event, during the dress rehearsal, Chanel lay on the floor checking the hem lengths of the models. When she was asked in late 1953 what she was expecting to create, Coco replied, 'How can you expect me to know? Until the last day I alter, transform. I create my dresses on the mannequins themselves.'[7]

As guests gathered in the grand salon, chattering with excitement as they took their seats on the reupholstered gilded chairs, Chanel was perched on the staircase, watching them like a hawk through the angles of the mirrors. She said, 'a collection is like a play: I hear the deathly silence in which a coat will pass, and have to take my cue'.

Those in the back rows stood on their chairs, and as the show began, a hush fell over the audience. The mannequins streamed out, each carrying a number. They were dressed in navy calf-length suits and straw boaters, lace gowns, mousseline dresses with artificial flowers, evening suits trimmed with gold brocade and schoolgirl coats.

But the audience looked unimpressed, and Chanel did not receive the reaction she had hoped for. Many critics were disappointed as it seemed old-fashioned, a ghost-like vision of her past. Chanel was devastated by the reaction, and old friends such as Maggie van Zuylen attempted to console her with their congratulations.

'The French fashion press lay in wait for her first postwar collection, like cats at a rat hole,' wrote Bettina Ballard. 'The blast in the press the next day was blindly violent, as if the fashion writers could in some way deny the strength of this voice from the past by ranting and raving.'

The critics saw it as repetition, old news compared to Dior, a 'sad retrospective' according to *L'Aurore* newspaper, with the article continuing: 'We were all rather moved. It was a whole past, virtually an epoch that we had been invited to watch coming back to life after fourteen years of silence. One felt somehow as if one were entering the palace of the Sleeping Beauty.' *Combat* newspaper's Lucien François was particularly brutal, describing her as 'this tireless, haughty, despotic little woman', and that 'Paris society turned out yesterday to devour the lion-tamer.'[8]

Even in Britain she couldn't escape the criticism. Ailsa Garland of *The Daily Mirror* said: 'The big question has been: Could she put on a show to compare with the masters of today? It is sad to say it – but she can't. She is designing for a world that is not of today. The publicity cannot harm the sale of the perfume and soap which have kept her name alive all these years. But as far as fashion goes, it was all rather sad.'[9]

While the French fashion press were vicious, perhaps as punishment for the rumours of her collaboration with the Germans, on the other side of the Atlantic Chanel was being praised for the easy wearability of her suits. *Vogue* highlighted 'a navy suit with squared shoulders (note the padding) a comfortable waistband, a tucked, buttoned-on blouse, a typical neck-bow, and a back of the head sailor hat' and 'an after-five dress in pink jersey with cleverly draped skirt, becoming V neck'.[10] A month later, in March 1954, *LIFE* magazine published a feature on Chanel's comeback, photographing the models on the Paris Métro, just as the designer had always primarily considered ease-of-movement for women in her designs.

Chanel recounted to Paul Morand: 'I am looking at a young woman on her bicycle, with her bag on her shoulders, one hand placed chastely on her knees that rise and fall, the material of her

The navy jersey suit, white blouse and straw boater, hailed by *Vogue* editor Bettina Ballard and modelled by Marie-Hélène Arnaud.

clothing cleaved to her stomach and chest, and her dress puffed up by the speed and the wind. This young woman has developed her own fashion, according to her needs, just as Crusoe built his hut; she is admirable and I admire her.'[11]

Bettina Ballard continued to be a Chanel faithful, and together with her assistant Susan Train and photographer Henry Clarke, she went to rue Cambon to select pieces from the collection. She chose the mid-calf navy jersey suit, worn with a white blouse and a straw boater by Marie-Hélène Arnaud during the show – a model who Chanel had shaped in her own image. It was an update of the prewar Chanel suit, and for Bettina it was a classic outfit that perfectly represented the modern woman. 'I wanted this costume for myself,' wrote Bettina. 'I had missed comfortable, reliably young clothes, like this, and I was sure that other women would want them, too, if they saw them.'[12]

American *Vogue* covered the Chanel Look of 1954, with Suzy

Parker modelling the navy suit, sailor hat and blouse, along with a draped, rose, wool-jersey dress and a navy strapless evening gown with roses. Suzy Parker was also on *Elle*'s cover in November 1954, wearing Chanel vermillion tweed. The magazine's editor, Lazareff, considered the style for the modern woman, 'for voting, wage-earning, independent women ... with no time to waste'.

By her next collection, in autumn 1954, Chanel had been rediscovered by the fashion press, and the Chanel Look was once again sought after. The navy suit and hat of her comeback inspired a new sailor trend in Paris, seen, according to British *Vogue*, 'in collars, colours, and a whole hands-in-pockets easiness to the line'.

She showed jersey suits and lace gowns in beige, wheat and grey, brightened with flashes of rose red and green. Yet some reporters were still not convinced of the style. Barbara Miller said: 'Her latest finely made gowns are perfect for women of a "certain age" – past 50 – but otherwise look strangely anachronistic in the bustling Paris of 1954. At her autumn show she used her timeless wool jerseys for suits and dresses, and stiff lace for evening ... typical lines of the perennial Chanel long-waisted casual silhouette can be summed up as high neckline, narrow inset shoulders, long and casually bloused belted waist, slightly flared and gored skirts with long mid-calf hemlines.'[13]

Each Chanel suit took 150 hours of work and they followed a similar format – soft tweed or jersey with luxurious silk linings, gilt braiding, grosgrain ribbon and buttons with a lion, star or camellia symbol. They were made from a crease-proof natural fabric, with the jacket cut like a cardigan, and the skirt featuring a ribbon stitched to the waistband to fix the blouse in place, a hidden chain in the silk lining of the hem to keep the shape, and slouchy pockets. Chanel thought of practical touches, such as a real pocket where a woman could keep her packet of cigarettes.[14]

Chanel personally chose each piece of fabric with a clear knowledge of its origins. She could tell whether a tweed had been made in the region of the River Tweed in the Scottish Borders, while Italian tweed felt too delicate and light-weight for her. Later, in the 1960s, Chanel selected soft boucle tweed from Scottish textile designer Bernat Klein for suits and dresses.[15] 'I make my dresses like a watch,' she said. 'If one tiny little wheel doesn't

Left: Bernat Klein tweed, inspired by the colours of a rose, featured by Chanel in a suit in her spring-summer 1963 collection.

Right: Chanel in her workrooms modelling a jersey suit and blouse, 1954.

work, I remake the dress. A dress isn't right if it is uncomfortable, if it doesn't "walk" properly … elegance in clothes means being able to move freely, to do anything with ease.'[16]

In February 1955, Chanel unveiled the 2.55 bag, named after its launch date, and it became an immediate classic. It was created with a hand-stitched diagonal pattern on soft quilted leather, a reference to the jackets of the Royallieu stable boys, coloured navy, beige, black and brown. Its defining feature was its golden metal chain strap with a leather cord. 'I got fed up with holding my purses in my hands and losing them,' she said. 'So I added a strap and carried them over my shoulder.'[17]

Also in the mid-1950s, Chanel launched another classic accessory: two-tone, slingback shoes made from beige kid with black toecaps, which helped create the illusion of a longer leg. These referenced fashionable men's shoes of the twenties, as worn by the Prince of Wales and the Duke of Westminster. Launched in 1957, the shoes were a practical answer to the stiletto, with their low heels to make it easier for walking.

By 1957, sales of Chanel suits had skyrocketed in America, and that year she visited the United States to collect an award. Before she returned to Paris, the *New Yorker* interviewed the dressmaker at New York's Waldorf Towers. She was dressed in a beige silk suit and straw hat, a white silk blouse, low-heeled brown and white shoes, ropes of pearls, a large, antique, gold brooch studded with rubies, emeralds and diamonds, and gold cufflinks that had been a gift from Stravinsky. 'We've met some formidable charmers in our time, but none to surpass the great couturière and perfumer Mlle. Gabrielle Chanel,' they wrote. 'At seventy-four Mlle. Chanel is sensationally good-looking, with dark brown eyes, a brilliant smile, and unquenching vitality of a twenty-year-old, and when, giving us a firm handshake, she said, "I am *très, très fatiguée*", it was with the assurance of a woman who knows she can afford to say it.'[18]

Model wearing a tweed suit and Chanel two-toned slingback shoes, around 1957. Chanel suits were for the active modern woman.

Chanel declared to the reporter, 'I am not interested any more in 1957. It is gone for me. I am more interested in 1958, 1959, 1960. Fashion is always of the time in which you live. It is not something standing alone. The problem of fashion in 1925 was different. Women were just beginning to go to work in offices. I inspired the cutting of the hair short because it goes with the modern woman. To the woman going to work, I said to take off the bone corset, because women cannot work while they are imprisoned in a corset. I invented the tweed for sports and the loose-fitting sweater and blouse … Nearly all women work, and if they don't work they want to work. So many women in France have a little car. They find it difficult to get in and out of the little car. This you cannot do with a crinoline skirt … today people travel a lot. The clothes must be light in weight for the flying. But the grand problem, the most important problem, is to rejuvenate women.'[19]

In Paris, Chanel welcomed some of the most famous women for fittings at her salon – Grace Kelly, Elizabeth Taylor, Lauren Bacall and Ingrid Bergman, for whom she created stage costumes for *Tea and Sympathy*. She also visited the home of Gerard Mille, France's great interior designer, who lived in a villa on rue de Varenne, popular with the new wave 1950s stars such as Marlon Brando, Brigitte Bardot, Roger Vadim and Juliette Gréco. Mille was inspired by Chanel's decor, also featuring Coromandel screens, mirrors, Venetian statues and baroque furnishings.[20]

She continued to invite guests to her rue Cambon apartment for dinner, often thought up at the last minute. As Claude Delay recalled: 'Her table served potatoes baked in embers and crackling in their silver foil; purée made of fresh chestnuts; as winter desserts, dates and figs mashed in cream.' When her biographer Marcel Haedrich first met Chanel in 1958, she was seventy-five years old and an intimidating figure who spoke with urgency. 'My first impression of her: an almost outrageously done-up old lady who talked endlessly.'[21]

She warmed herself by the fire with sips of vodka, favouring it because it was made from wheat.[22] When she received flowers from people she didn't like, she had them taken into another room, which she called the cemetery. That fate happened to Richard Avedon in 1959, as he had photographed Audrey Hepburn for *Harper's Bazaar*, wearing another of Chanel's young rivals, Givenchy.

11

The Twilight Years

'The opposite of luxury is not necessarily poverty: it is hats and skirt lengths that go out of style.'

Lausanne, Switzerland
1966–1971

In the 1960s, Coco Chanel continued to compete with the younger designers, but the decade was difficult for her. It was the era of the 'youthquake' and fashion was rising from the streets, reflecting what young people were wearing in London's Carnaby Street or on the King's Road. Mary Quant designed the miniskirt, Paco Rabanne experimented with plastic and chainmail and André Courrèges was taking Paris by storm with his futuristic designs. Courrèges said: 'I am the Matra, the Ferrari, Chanel is the Rolls-Royce: functional but static.'

Regardless of the criticism that she was no longer innovative, Chanel remained faithful to her silhouette, and to comforting details, such as luxury linings. 'Linings – there's the secret: linings and cut. Courrèges doesn't line anything,' she said. 'The opposite of luxury is not necessarily poverty: it is hats and skirt lengths that go out of style.' And this was why she kept on producing her classics.[1]

Chanel felt it was her duty to women to make clothes the way she always had. 'Men make dresses in which one can't move. They tell you very calmly that the dresses aren't made for action. I'm frightened when I hear such things. What will happen when no one else thinks as I do anymore? I told my girls: "I'm going to die, listen to me. I'm teaching you something very important. Don't stand there looking like such dopes!"'[2]

While Yves Saint Laurent was dressing women in black leather for his Beat collection, Chanel continued her reliable look of soft tweed suits with braiding, knee-length pleated skirts, navy dresses with starched white collars and cuffs.[253] Despite the traditional nature of her designs, she attracted to her salon the hip young fashion icons – Catherine Deneuve, Jeanne Moreau, Anouk Aimée and Romy Schneider.

British fashion journalist Felicity Green, in July 1963, wrote of Chanel 'dishing up the latest of the Chanel Look. Which you'll be glad to know, differs only slightly from the previous Chanel Look. There was once a rumour that Chanel had changed her ideas completely. But it turned out to be merely that she had used a different type of braid binding … and the panic was over.'[3]

Austrian actress Romy Schneider being fitted by Chanel at the rue Cambon salon in 1960.

In a 1969 interview with French TV presenter Micheline Sandrel, words rolled out of Chanel in a stream of consciousness on the stupidity of modern life, and in particular the miniskirt. 'I've been fighting all couturiers for the past two years on those shorts dresses. I find them indecent. It's not in the time you know. To show one's knees, they need to be perfect, they are an articulation, it's like showing your elbow ... I've got nothing against knees if they're pretty. But if they're not pretty, if you stand on rue Cambon all day long, you'll struggle to find people with good legs.'[4]

She also took aim at the social habits of Parisians. 'Paris is losing its prestige,' she said. 'It's becoming vulgar whereas it didn't use to be. It used to be ravishing. There should be some protocol for dinner time ... Everything is going south in France, you invite people for dinner at 8p.m., they turn up at 10p.m. and can't see what's wrong with it.'[5]

Having spent many years at Lausanne's Hôtel Beau Rivage, in 1966 Chanel rented a house on the outskirts of the Swiss city called Villa Le Signal, at 20 route du Signal, surrounded by the lush green Sauvabelin woods. Rather than living on the shores of Lake Geneva she chose to be closer to the mountains, as she found the waters of the lake 'appalling, with swans that smell awful. The marsh hens are dying off – the water's polluted.' Like her home on the Riviera, it demonstrated her preference for clean mountain air and steep climbs rather than being on the shoreline. Chanel's home was opposite a former stop for the mountain railway, where mansions and luxurious chalets could enjoy the quiet peacefulness of Alpine woods.

Lausanne has a long connection with celebrity, with Lord Byron and Percy Shelley passing through on their tour of Lake Geneva in 1816, and Charles Dickens and his family staying for six months in 1846. The mountain air felt restorative to those who breathed it, and the backdrop of lake, snow-covered mountains and green pastures offered soul-cleansing views.

Chanel's friend Jean Cocteau painted and exhibited in Lausanne. He wrote that 'To talk of Lausanne is to talk of my youth and my heart ... Everything I get from Lausanne comes from a place where the air that you breathe is the air of the soul.'

Audrey Hepburn resided in Switzerland at the same time as Chanel, living in a large farmhouse called La Paisible, thirty minutes from Lausanne, while Charlie Chaplin inhabited a generous mansion with mountain views in Vevey, where Chanel's friend Paul Morand also lived. It was in Chanel's ornamental salon at Le Signal that Morand interviewed her on her life, producing a work that was published after her death as L'Allure de Chanel.

Chanel moved into Villa Le Signal on 12 January 1966 and was a tenant of Mr Cohen Sabetay; she never purchased the home outright. In 1960, she had made a bid to buy a neighbouring house, Château du Signal, at 22 route du Signal. But its owner, the publisher Albert Mermoud, refused her offer. David Bowie bought

Chanel's Swiss chalet, Villa
Le Signal, in the Sauvabelin
woods, outside of Lausanne.

the château later, in 1982, as a creative retreat, where he
recorded the single *Let's Dance* with Nile Rodgers.[6]

Chanel called her Swiss home 'the little suburban villa', and
proclaimed that 'these days one can't live in a house that
requires more than two servants. I want something small, a nest,
where I can relax until I die. It's a very comfortable house – water
and heat are in, I don't have to do anything. I have three
bathrooms and a shower, not to mention my own bathroom.
Inside I'll do the walls in lacquered things; the outside, since it's
Switzerland, I'll do in chalet style.'[7]

She loved the smell of the forest; the snow reminded her of St
Moritz, and her garden, with its ancient sequoia tree, offered
relaxation. She imported turf from Britain to even out the garden,
as she had done with the garden at Rue du Faubourg Saint-
Honoré.[8]

She painted her tin staircase black, so 'it'll disappear into the
atmosphere', while her wrought-iron bed and chairs were
created by the brother of sculptor Alberto Giacometti. 'It'll be a
house of iron that can't be eaten up by moths!' she declared. In
the bedrooms, instead of warm eiderdowns, her camp beds were
covered in the wild sheepskin of her childhood. 'You get hot, you
throw it on the floor, and in the morning you have to clutch it back
again.' But she told Claude Delay that she still had plans to 'dress'

Chanel and her
mannequins,
backstage 1962.

her house. In the snow, she said, 'it was a bit unreal. There's no linen in it yet. No life.'[9]

Her chauffeur would take her to visit the Chalet-des-Enfants de Sauvabelin, or whisk her down to Lausanne's lakefront for dinner at the Hôtel Beau Rivage, or sometimes she would stay there when she felt too crowded and bored from the guests in her house, playing cards by the fire. 'I camp in Lausanne as I do in Paris. You know I never settle down anywhere. I've chosen freedom!' [10]

Back in Paris, when preparing for her twice-yearly collections, Chanel continued to live permanently at the Hôtel Ritz, making the short journey to rue Cambon every day. 'I've always lived in attics or palaces. I don't want any more palaces, but I do like to keep a good table.'

Coco had the devotion of her young, beautiful mannequins, the girls who admired and looked up to her, and who, like Suzy Parker, she could shape in her image. She was also attended by a select group of staff in her later years. François Mironnet, her butler, was from Normandy and it was remarked that he resembled the Duke of Westminster. She trusted him to take care of her jewellery and to keep her company during dinners at the Ritz as she was lonely and sought a man for conversation. He assisted her in climbing the stairs, and handed her glasses of water to take her pills. Her maid, who she called Jeanne, kept her living quarters and her clothes in order.[11]

Another companion in her later years was Claude Delay, who would write several books on Chanel, including *Chanel Solitaire*, and who acted as confidante and witnessed her daily schedule. Chanel woke at 7.30a.m., enjoying a leisurely breakfast of porridge, coffee and cigarettes, dressed in white silk men's pyjamas, just as she had when bombs fell on the city in the First World War. A stylist from Guillame hair salon would arrive at 9a.m. to fix her hair and secure the straw boater, while she talked and gossiped incessantly over the phone.

A make-up artist painted her mouth a slash of red, and her skin, including that of her hands, was tinted. Sometimes this tint would rub off on her white cuffs, so she ensured she had extra pairs of cuffs to change into. A gardenia on the lapel of her beige suit and a spray of Chanel N°.5 to scent her clothes were the finishing touches.[12]

As Claude recalled, 'She was so intense, so riveting in her despotic little boater, emerging from her mirrored stairway, that I dimly caught her essential aroma, and the even more illicit scent of eternal youth.'

Chanel often went for drives in Paris up the Champs Élysées and around her old Paris haunts. Passing the Bois de Boulogne, she reminisced – 'There used to be men who played polo madly all day, reeking of horses. That's all over now.' Driving through Ville d'Avray she remembered meeting Matisse there. 'Like all real artists – you didn't notice him.'[13]

In her later years, Chanel often instructed her chauffeur to drive her through the streets of Paris.

She said that 'Paris in July is delightful. Everything is lovely and empty, the Parisians who are there for the day have left. One has the city to oneself.' Sometimes she would go for walks at the Père Lachaise cemetery, along the rambling, quiet paths by the gravestones.[14]

She then made the short journey to the salon, where she would have a leisurely lunch at 1p.m. with friends. She fastened her skirt with a safety pin to ensure she was comfortable after eating, as she wouldn't return to the Ritz until the evening. From the upstairs workrooms, they could tell when she arrived just by smelling the air. There were times when she wouldn't make an appearance in the workroom until 5p.m., which sent her assistants into a panic, as they had all been ready to go home for the day. Her seamstresses worked into the evening, addressing her whims in the same manner. 'Yes, Mademoiselle, very well, Mademoiselle.'[15]

Chanel's premiere, Madame Raymonde, placed the scissors on a ribbon around Chanel's neck, and as Coco worked, she fitted the dress to the model, running her hand over her to check the way the fabric sat, snipping with her scissors, and with pins, buttons and ribbons all within her reach. The classic image of Coco Chanel in her twilight years is with a cigarette hanging from her mouth like a prop, a look of concentration on her face as she pinched the fabric to check the fit and the fall. 'I don't know how to sew; I do know where to stick pins in,' she told Marcel Haedrich. 'I take care of the inside of my fingers. In my work I don't need anything else. I was very skilful, I did whatever I wanted with my hands.'[16]

By 8p.m. she was finished and returned to the Ritz for dinner at her usual table at the lobby entrance to the dining room, so she could be seen and observe those who were coming in. By eating lightly, she ensured her weight stayed the same throughout her life – 'cut off my head and I'm still thirteen'. Chanel's age was a mystery up until her death. When a young American journalist attempted a quick-fire interview in 1959, he made the mistake of asking her age. 'My age varies according to the days and the people I happen to be with. When I'm bored I feel very old, and since I'm extremely bored with you, I'm going to be a thousand years old in five minutes …'[17]

Chanel's collection in 1968 was attended by stars such as Lauren Bacall, yet she was 'gambling on Chanel modesty', with knee-length skirts in Scottish tweed, but the collection failed to make a splash. Gloria Emerson of the *New York Times* commented

Wool coat with stripes and oversized pockets, 1964, and cream wool suit with navy stripes and blouse, 1962, define the Chanel uniform style of the 1960s.

Katharine Hepburn in the
Broadway production
of *Coco* in 1969.

on the museum-like pieces she created in the 1960s, where
'Chanel's long skirts that ended below the knees seemed a joke in
a world that was mad for minis. The long, languid lines of her suits
and coats had too much marshmallow and not enough snap.'[18]

Chanel had been reluctant for her life to be exposed and
dissected, but she agreed to a musical comedy by André Previn
and Alan Jay Lerner after first meeting producer Frederick Brisson
in Paris in 1958. The plans took almost a decade, and with
Beaton's designs for *My Fair Lady* in mind, Chanel had imagined
Audrey Hepburn playing her at the belle époque racecourses of
Deauville and Longchamps, surrounded by frothy lilac and
cream gowns. In fact, Katharine Hepburn was cast in the role,
encapsulating the essence of Coco. They both unashamedly
wore trousers in the 1930s, they had that same indomitable
no-nonsense attitude, and in the 1960s, they were considered
grandes dames.

Cecil Beaton visited rue Cambon in April 1965 for preparations
for *Coco*. 'The mirrored palaces below were now heavily
populated. The apartment upstairs more than ever filled with
glitter of gold lacquer, ormolu and crystal … Chanel in oatmeal
with facings of crimson and navy blue, looked thinner, but

otherwise of an extraordinary girlishness. She was talking her head off to her staff.'

They lunched at the Ritz, and he observed: 'Her eyes like pansies, with dark heavy lashes, her skin very clean and her aura delightfully perfumed, with hands that are like a peasant's. She kept fluttering a pair of gloves and I noticed that only the hands had become old.'[19]

Despite her reservations of seeing her life on stage, Chanel was looking forward to the premiere in New York, and she created a dazzling white sequinned gown especially for the occasion. She also planned to launch a new perfume in honour of the musical, called *Coco*, which she had developed twenty years before and had rediscovered the recipe. The week before she was set to leave for New York, Chanel alarmingly suffered sudden nerve damage in her right arm, losing all function in it. Instead of attending the premiere she chose to stay in Paris to struggle on with her next collection.

Following the success of *Coco* on Broadway, a huge crowd gathered at rue Cambon for Chanel's Spring-Summer 1970 show. As Gloria Emerson noted, Chanel 'strode right back into fashion today. The elderly couturière probably did not even know she was ever out of it. After all, for Chanel there is only Chanel.'

Chanel had refused to drop or raise the hemline, stubbornly keeping it just below the knee. But for the 1970s, with fatigue for the mod miniskirt and the flowing maxi skirts of the hippie era, it was just right. 'One of the dresses that drew raves in this January 1970 – even from the maxi-skirted youngsters who are not Chanel fans – is a white silk, splattered with navy polka dots, which has a side closing on top and a very pleated skirt. That Peter Pan collar with the tiny navy bow tie might have looked corny last year but, oh, not now, when fashions are getting sweeter,' wrote Emerson.[20]

Her models were dressed in red, white and beige plaids, jackets with low pockets and rounded necklines and gold buttons, accessorised with the classic beige and black slingback shoes, pearl earrings and a big, soft bow tying back the hair.[21]

Sydney Gittler and Irene Satz of Ohrbach's, the first store to make Chanel copies in 1954, thought her new collection was 'perfect for this moment in fashion'.[22] By the close of 1970, Chanel's sales had risen 30 per cent in Paris year-on-year. Her clothes continued to be championed by Marlene Dietrich and Catherine Deneuve, and Coco was riding on a wave of success with a simple ankle-length black dress in silk organza. 'Two years ago, a dress like this would have looked like Old Alabama but it should be a best seller now,' said Marcel Haedrich. The praise for Chanel continued for her autumn-winter 1970 collection, shown in July of that year.[23]

While she worked as hard as ever at rue Cambon, every time Chanel made her way up the mirrored staircase, she had to stop for breath on a particular step. 'That step is well known by now,'

Coco Chanel chose
to observe her shows
from the mirrored
staircase of her salon.

said her shop supervisor Madame Raymonde. She was finding new bruises and suffering stiff joints, arthritis, broken or sore ribs. 'I fell out of bed again,' she said. 'To prevent it the table had been moved against the bed, but that's not enough anymore. I'm going to have my mattress put on the floor; that way, at least, I won't have so far to fall.'[24]

Her sleepwalking had come back – she remembered being six years old and her father putting her back in bed again, but now she would wake up in the corridors of the Ritz. The woman who had told the *New Yorker* in 1957 when she was seventy-four years old: 'I am not young, but I feel young. The day I feel old, I will go to bed and stay there.'

On Sunday 10 January 1971, Chanel lunched with Claude Delay at the Ritz, then the two of them took a drive along the Champs-Élysées in the stark winter sunshine. She was in the middle of finishing her latest collection, with only weeks to go. Returning to the Ritz for dinner, she said goodbye to Claude at the entrance and returned to her room. Once there, she struggled to catch her breath and asked her maid Jeanne to open the window to try and ease her feeling of suffocation. As she lay down on the bed Gabrielle Chanel uttered her final words, 'So this is how one dies.' Jeanne placed her under the white sheets of her bed, dressing her in a white suit and blouse.

When Chanel talked of her childhood, it was always in winter – the snow, the roaring fires – rather than spring or summer, with their rebirth and rainstorms, and so it was perhaps fitting that she died in January. Her funeral service was held at L'Église de la Madeleine, attended by hundreds of Parisians, and seated in the front were six of her models, dressed in Chanel tweed suits. As a floral tribute, white camellias formed a pair of scissors, with the words 'To Mademoiselle from her mannequins'. Another wreath of white camellias and white orchids came from producer Frederick Brisson, while a bunch of blood-red roses slashed through the white flowers on her coffin.[25] Chanel had requested that her body be taken back to Switzerland, where the headstone of her marble vault in the cemetery of Bois-de-Vaux in Lausanne has five lions carved on it and a simple cross with her name.

Writing for *The Guardian* newspaper just after Chanel's death, Alison Adburgham lamented: 'It is sad that Chanel should have died just two weeks before the Paris Spring Collections begin. This could have been the moment in fashion history when Gabrielle (Coco) Chanel, who was eighty-seven years old, could have made the look for the third time round ... in 1971, one could anticipate a third Chanel period, a reaction to normality after the extremes of mini and maxi.'[26]

As it was, 25 January 1971 was the first Chanel show without Mademoiselle, and she was missed. In the audience was Claude Pompidou, wife of French president Georges Pompidou, in a black Chanel suit.[25] Claude Pompidou had been Chanel's client and admirer for many years, and when the designer was invited for dinner at the presidential home at the Élysée Palace, Chanel had remarked, 'In my day one did not invite one's dressmaker for dinner.'

As the first pale tweed suit appeared from the staircase, the audience quietened, and mannequins filed past in further tweeds, coats and white evening dresses, with their hair tied in knots and fastened with a black bow for mourning. The audience clapped loudly at its conclusion, glancing at the staircase, almost as if they expected Chanel to make one last appearance before her crowd.

All her life, Gabrielle Chanel had sought freedom from the poverty and restraints of her childhood at the convent at Aubazine. Emerging at a time of circumstances that allowed for women to be more independent, she designed clothes that endorsed that freedom as women played sports, drove cars and rode bicycles, and went to work. And as she found fame and love and success, she used the memories of her past, and the way that she had lived, to forge her own independence.

Endnotes

Chapter 1: The Country Girl

1. Claude Baillen, *Chanel Solitaire*, translated by Barbara Bay, Collins, 1973, p167.
2. Cévennes Mont-Lozère, Office due Tourisme de Genolhac.
3. Isabelle Fiemeyer and Gabrielle Palasse-Labrunie, *Intimate Chanel*, Flammarion, 2011, p18.
4. Marcel Haedrich, *Coco Chanel: Her Life, Her Secrets*, Little Brown and Company, 1972, p20.
5. Edmonde Charles-Roux, *Chanel and her World*, Weidenfeld and Nicolson, 1979, p26.
6. Paul Morand, *The Allure of Chanel*, Pushkin Collection, 2013.
7. Morand, *The Allure*.
8. Axel Madsen, *Coco Chanel: A Biography*, Bloomsbury, 1990, p11.
9. Haedrich, *Her Life, Her Secrets*, p25.
10. Morand, *The Allure*.
11. Barriére, Bernadette, Aubazine: Obazine-Croyeux, a double monastery, Association Harpau, 2009.
12. Madsen, *A Biography*, p14.
13. Haedrich, *Her Life, Her Secrets*, p30.
14. Barriére, Bernadette, Aubazine: Obazine-Croyeux, a double monastery.
15. Barriére, Bernadette, Aubazine: Obazine-Croyeux, a double monastery.
16. Haedrich, *Her Life, Her Secrets*, p29.
17. Morand, *The Allure*.
18. Morand, *The Allure*.
19. Charles-Roux, *Chanel and her World*, p30.
20. Lisa Chaney, *Chanel: An Intimate Life*, Penguin, 2011.
21. Madsen, *A Biography*, p23.
22. Haedrich, *Her Life, Her Secrets*, p49.
23. https://www.detoursenfrance.fr/ patrimoine/personnages-celebres/ moulins-sur-les-pas-de-coco-chanel-3296
24. Haedrich, *Her Life, Her Secrets*, p57.
25. Haedrich, *Her Life, Her Secrets*, p51.
26. Haedrich, *Her Life, Her Secrets*, p22.
27. Morand, *The Allure*.
28. Charles-Roux, *Chanel and her World*, p45.
29. Chaney, *An Intimate Life*.
30. Haedrich, *Her Life, Her Secrets*, p61.
31. Madsen, *A Biography*, p40.
32. Haedrich, *Her Life, Her Secrets*, p64.
33. Morand, *The Allure*.
34. Haedrich, *Her Life, Her Secrets*, p69.
35. Baillen, *Chanel Solitaire*, p23.
36. Morand, *The Allure*.

Chapter 2: Genre Pauvre

1. http://www.chanel-muggeridge.com/ unpublished-interview/
2. Morand, *The Allure*.
3. Haedrich, *Her Life, Her Secrets*, p72.
4. Morand, *The Allure*.
5. Baillen, *Chanel Solitaire*, p180.
6. Haedrich, *Her Life, Her Secrets*, p64.
7. Baillen, *Chanel Solitaire*, p20.
8. Bronwyn Cosgrave, *Vogue on Coco Chanel*, Quadrille Publishing, p18.
9. *Mlle Lucienne Roger dans le Mariage de Mlle Beulemans*, Comoedia Illustré, 15 September 1910.
10. *La Mode actuelle au Theatre*, Comoedia Illustré, 1 October 1910.
11. Madsen, *A Biography*, p58.
12. Charles-Roux, *Chanel and her World*, p72.
13. Madsen, *A Biography*, p56.
14. Baillen, *Chanel Solitaire*.
15. Baillen, *Chanel Solitaire*.
16. Morand, *The Allure*.
17. Morand, *The Allure*.
18. Haedrich, *Her Life, Her Secrets*, p75.
19. Justine Picardie, *Coco Chanel: The Legend and the Life*, HarperCollins, 2010.
20. Madsen, *A Biography*, p53.
21. Madsen, *A Biography*, p61.
22. 'What Fashionable Folk are Wearing at Deauville', *New York Times*, 21 September 1913.
23. 'What Fashionable Folk are Wearing'.
24. 'What Fashionable Folk are Wearing'.
25. Madsen, *A Biography*, p59.

26. *Women's Wear Daily*, July 1915.
27. Madsen, *A Biography*, p66.
28. Morand, *The Allure*.
29. Madsen, *A Biography*, p76.
30. British *Vogue*, September 1917.
31. Morand, *The Allure*.
32. Haedrich, *Her Life, Her Secrets*, p96.
33. Chaney, *An Intimate Life*.
34. Charles-Roux, *Chanel and her World*, p99.
35. British *Vogue*, 1 July 1916.
36. British *Vogue*, 15 September 1916.
37. Morand, *The Allure*.
38. Madsen, *A Biography*, p80.
39. Amy de la Haye, *Chanel: Couture and Industry*, V & A Publishing, 2011, p31.
40. Morand, *The Allure*.
41. British *Vogue*, early August, 1919.
42. Haedrich, *Her Life, Her Secrets*, p175.
43. British *Vogue*, early August, 1919.
44. John Julius Norwich, *The Duff Cooper Diaries*, 1915–1951, Weidenfeld & Nicolson, 2014.
45. 'English Motorist Killed in France', *The Times*, 24 December 1919.
46. Chaney, *An Intimate Life*.
47. Morand, *The Allure*.

Chapter 3: Bohemian Paris

1. Morand, *The Allure*.
2. Morand, *The Allure*.
3. Morand, *The Allure*.
4. Haedrich, *Her Life, Her Secrets*, p101.
5. Morand, *The Allure*.
6. Morand, *The Allure*.
7. Morand, *The Allure*.
8. Baillen, *Chanel Solitaire*. p49.
9. Justine Picardie, *The Legend and the Life*.
10. Madsen, *A Biography*, p92.
11. Chaney, *An Intimate Life*.
12. Charles-Roux, *Chanel and her World*, p170.
13. Robert Craft, *Stravinsky: Selected correspondence*, 1982, Faber and Faber Ltd.
14. Justine Picardie, *The Legend and the Life*.

15. Justine Picardie, *The Legend and the Life*.
16. Amy de la Haye, *Couture and Industry*, p51.
17. Chaney, *An Intimate Life*.
18. Robert Craft, *Stravinsky*.
19. Morand, *The Allure*.
20. British *Vogue*, March 1922.
21. Morand, *The Allure*.
22. May Birkhead, 'Chanel entertains at brilliant fete', *New York Times*, 5 July 1931.
23. Morand, *The Allure*.
24. Baillen, *Chanel Solitaire*, p49.
25. Morand, *The Allure*.
26. Madsen, *A Biography*, p128.
27. Chaney, *An Intimate Life*.
28. 'Wide skirts rule in Paris fashion', *New York Times*, 4 August 1924.
29. American *Vogue*, October 1926.
30. Morand, *The Allure*.
31. Haedrich, *Her Life, Her Secrets*, p119.
32. Chaney, *An Intimate Life*.
33. Haedrich, *Her Life, Her Secrets*, p118.

Chapter 4: Rue Cambon

1. Amy de la Haye, *Couture and Industry*, p38.
2. Haedrich, *Her Life, Her Secrets*.
3. Janet Flanner, '31 Rue Cambon', *New Yorker*, 14 March 1931.
4. Bettina Ballard, *In My Fashion*, V & A Perspectives, 2017.
5. Bettina Ballard, *In My Fashion*.
6. Haedrich, *Her Life, Her Secrets*, p183.

Chapter 5: The Scent of Success

1. Justine Picardie, *The Legend and the Life*.
2. Chaney, *An Intimate Life*.
3. Ernest Beaux, 'Memories of a Perfumer', *Industrie de la Parfumerie*, (boisdejasmin.com)
4. Lauren Collins, 'Fragrant Harvest', *New Yorker*. March 19 2018.
5. Chaney, *An Intimate Life*.
6. Misia Sert, *Two or Three Muses*, Museum Press, 1953.
7. Chaney, *An Intimate Life*.

8. Haedrich, *Her Life, Her Secrets*, p16.
9. Bettina Ballard, *In My Fashion*.

Chapter 6: The British Look

1. Amy de la Haye, *Couture and Industry*, p19.
2. Madsen, *A Biography*, p145.
3. Morand, *The Allure*.
4. Winston and Clementine Churchill, *Speaking for Themselves: The Personal Letters of Winston Churchill*, Black Swan, 1999.
5. Haedrich, *Her Life, Her Secrets*, p125.
6. Baillen, *Chanel Solitaire*, p44.
7. Morand, *The Allure*.
8. Madsen, *A Biography*, p154.
9. Baillen, *Chanel Solitaire*, p46.
10. Sudouest.fr, *The Summer of the Landes Coco Chanel*, 20 July 2010.
11. Churchill, *Speaking for Themselves*.
12. Morand, *The Allure*.
13. Morand, *The Allure*.
14. Morand, *The Allure*.
15. Haedrich, *Her Life, Her Secrets*, p126.
16. Haedrich, *Her Life, Her Secrets*, p126.
17. Churchill, *Speaking for Themselves*.
18. Baillen, *Chanel Solitaire*, p44.
19. Iain Cram, Interview on Rosehall.
20. Iain Cram, Interview.
21. Churchill, *Speaking for Themselves*.
22. Patricia M. Hitchon, *Chanel and the Tweedmaker: Weaver of Dreams*, P3 Publications, September 2012.
23. Morand, *The Allure*.
24. Patricia M. Hitchon, *Chanel and the Tweedmaker*.
25. British *Vogue*, June 1927, 'Chanel Opens Her London House'.
26. 'MME Chanel Duke's Guest', *New York Times*, 18 November 1928.
27. Haedrich, *Her Life, Her Secrets*, p130.
28. Madsen, *A Biography*, p183.
29. Morand, *The Allure*.
30. Justine Picardie, *The Legend and the Life*.

Chapter 7: Riviera Chic

1. Bettina Ballard, *In My Fashion*.
2. F. Scott Fitzgerald, *Tender is the Night*, Scribner, 2003, p327.

3. Morand, *The Allure*.
4. Madsen, *A Biography*, p170.
5. Madsen, *A Biography*, p171.
6. Bronwyn Cosgrave, *Vogue on Coco Chanel*, p109.
7. May Birkhead, 'No. 17, Favorite at Monte Carlo', *New York Times*, 26 February 1926.
8. Oliver Meslay/Martha MacLeod, *From Chanel to Reves: La Pausa and Its Collections at the Dallas Museum of Art*, Dallas Museum of Art, p8.
9. Baillen, *Chanel Solitaire*, p111.
10. *La Simplicité Moderne*, French *Vogue*, May 1930.
11. Bettina Ballard, *In My Fashion*.
12. Jody Shields, 'The Queen of Clean', *New York Times*, 11 October 1992.
13. Morand, *The Allure*.
14. Paris Formal Pajamas Adopt Tailored Trousers, *New York Times*, 5 July, 1931.
15. Meslay/MacLeod, *From Chanel to Reves*, p16.
16. Vivian Russell, *Gardens of the Riviera*, Random House, 1994.
17. Madsen, *A Biography*, p170.
18. Bettina Ballard, *In My Fashion*.
19. Bettina Ballard, *In My Fashion*.
20. Bettina Ballard, *In My Fashion*.
21. Bettina Ballard, *In My Fashion*.
22. Baillen, *Chanel Solitaire*, p112.
23. Chaney, *An Intimate Life*.
24. Meslay/MacLeod, *From Chanel to Reves*, p23.
25. Meslay/MacLeod, *From Chanel to Reves*, p7.

Chapter 8: Chanel in the 1930s

1. Loelia Mary Grosvenor, *Grace and Favour: The Memoirs of Loelia Duchess of Westminster*, Leicester, 1967.
2. Madsen, *A Biography*, p172.
3. Fiemeyer and Palasse-Labrunie, *Intimate Chanel*, p93.
4. Diana Vreeland, *DV*, Vintage Books, 1985.
5. French *Vogue*, February 1930.
6. 'A Quoi Revent Les Jeunes Filles', French *Vogue*, June 1930.

7. http://inside.chanel.com/en/ timeline/1932_bijoux-de-diamants

8. Gloria Swanson, *Swanson on Swanson*, Random House, 1981.

9. Janet Flanner, '31 Rue Cambon', *New Yorker*, 14 March 1931.

10. Bettina Ballard, *In My Fashion*.

11. Morand, *The Allure*.

12. '*Le Mesnil Guillaume*', French *Vogue*, September 1930.

13. '*Le Mesnil Guillaume*', French *Vogue*, September 1930.

14. '*Chanel Robes*', French *Vogue*, February 1931.

15. Morand, *The Allure*.

16. Morand, *The Allure*.

17. Morand, *The Allure*.

18. Elsa Schiaparelli, *Shocking Life, The Autobiography of Elsa Schiaparelli*, V & A Fashion Perspectives, 2007.

19. Vreeland, *DV*.

20. Madsen, *A Biography*, p160.

21. British *Vogue*, July 1938.

22. Bettina Ballard, *In My Fashion*.

23. Chaney, *An Intimate Life*.

24. British *Vogue*, September 1939.

Chapter 9: At the Ritz

1. Baillen, Claude, *Chanel Solitaire*, translated by Barbara Bay, Collins, 1973, p108

2. Tilar J. Mazzeo, *The Hotel on Place Vendôme*, Harper, 2014.

3. Tilar J. Mazzeo, *The Hotel on Place Vendôme*.

4. Madsen, *A Biography*, p199.

5. Bettina Ballard, *In My Fashion*.

6. Tilar J. Mazzeo, *The Hotel on Place Vendôme*.

7. Cole Lesley, *Remembered Laughter: The Life of Noël Coward*, Knopf, 1976.

8. Justine Picardie, *The Legend and the Life*.

9. Justine Picardie, *The Legend and the Life*.

10. Tilar J. Mazzeo, *The Hotel on Place Vendôme*.

11. Hal Vaughan, *Sleeping with the Enemy: Coco Chanel, Nazi Agent*, Vintage, 2011.

12. Justine Picardie, *The Legend and the Life*.

13. Vaughan, *Sleeping with the Enemy*.

14. http://www.chanel-muggeridge.com/ unpublished-interview/

15. Baillen, *Chanel Solitaire*, p108.

16. Alexander Fury, 'Chanel's Ritzy Ode to Parisian Society', *New York Times*, 7 December 2016.

17. Fiemeyer and Palasse-Labrunie, *Intimate Chanel*, p163.

18. 'Paris Notes: A Chic Tree For Chanel', *New York Times*, 25 December 1963.

Chapter 10: The Comeback

1. Registrations, Ville de Lausanne archives.

2. Bronwyn Cosgrave, *Vogue on Coco Chanel*, p129.

3. Lillian Ross, 'The Strong Ones', *New Yorker*, 28 September 1957.

4. Justine Picardie, *The Legend and the Life*.

5. Rosamond Bernier, 'The Return of Chanel', British *Vogue*, February 1954.

6. Rosamond Bernier, 'The Return of Chanel'.

7. Chaney, *An Intimate Life*.

8. Haedrich, *Her Life, Her Secrets*, p169.

9. Ailsa Garland, 'Chanel brings a whiff of the past', *Daily Mirror*, 6 February 1954.

10. British *Vogue*, March 1954.

11. Morand, *The Allure*.

12. Bettina Ballard, *In My Fashion*.

13. Barbara Miller, 'Old and New', *Derry Journal*, 25 October 1954.

14. Baillen, *Chanel Solitaire*, p58.

15. Baillen, *Chanel Solitaire*, p64.

16. Rosamond Bernier, 'The Return of Chanel', British *Vogue*, February 1954.

17. Justine Picardie, *The Legend and the Life*.

18. Ross, 'The Strong Ones'.

19. Ross, 'The Strong Ones'.

20. Haedrich, *Her Life, Her Secrets*, p206.

21. Baillen, *Chanel Solitaire*, p15.

22. Haedrich, *Her Life, Her Secrets*, p3.

Chapter 11: The Twilight Years

1. Haedrich, *Her Life, Her Secrets*, p253.

2. Haedrich, *Her Life, Her Secrets*, p245.

3. Felicity Green, 'The Face that Launched a Million Suits', *Daily Mirror*, 16 August 1962.

4. Felicity Green, 'Hot Momma', *Daily Mirror*, 30 July 1963.

5. http://fashionabecedaire.tumblr.com/ post/16695026717/interview-translation- coco-chanel-on-fame

6. http://fashionabecedaire.tumblr.com/ post/16695026717/interview-translation- coco-chanel-on-fame

7. Registrations, Ville de Lausanne archives.

8. Baillen, *Chanel Solitaire*, p112.

9. Baillen, *Chanel Solitaire*, p112.

10. Baillen, *Chanel Solitaire*, p112.

11. Baillen, *Chanel Solitaire*, p114.

12. Haedrich, *Her Life, Her Secrets*, p256.

13. Angela Taylor, 'Shades of Chanel: A Remake From Paris', *New York Times*, 11 September, 1976.

14. Baillen, *Chanel Solitaire*, p161.

15. Justine Picardie, *The Legend and the Life*.

16. Haedrich, *Her Life, Her Secrets*, p245.

17. Haedrich, *Her Life, Her Secrets*, p241.

18. Haedrich, *Her Life, Her Secrets*, p215.

19. Gloria Emerson, 'Fashion Steps Back and Catches Up to Chanel', *New York Times*, 30 January 1970.

20. Cecil Beaton, *Beaton in the Sixties: The Cecil Beaton Diaries as he Wrote Them, 1965–1969*, Alfred A Knopf, 2004.

21. Gloria Emerson, 'Fashion Steps Back'.

22. Gloria Emerson, 'Fashion Steps Back'.

23. Gloria Emerson, 'Fashion Steps Back'.

24. Gloria Emerson, 'Fashion Steps Back'.

25. Haedrich, *Her Life, Her Secrets*, p223.

26. Justine Picardie, *The Legend and the Life*.

27. Alison Adburgham, 'In Loco Coco', *The Guardian*, 12 January 1971.

28. 'Coco is missed', *New York Times*, 27 January 1971.

Picture credits

The publishers would like to thank all those listed below for permission to reproduce the images. Every care has been taken to trace copyright holders. Any copyright holders we have been unable to reach are invited to contact the publishers so that a full acknowledgement may be given in subsequent editions.

The Advertising Archives: 87

akg-images/Schutze/Rodemann: 113

Alamy 6 (Francois Roux); 16 (Herve Lenain); 31 (Historic Collection); 34 (Allstar Picture Library); 50 (Lordprice Collection); 88 right (Heritage Image Partnership Ltd/ Photograph by Fine Art Images); 99 (imageBROKER/Photograph by Markus Keller); 104-5 (Andrew Ray); 125 (Granger Historical Picture Archive)

Bridgeman Art Museum: 32, 55, 98 (Tallandier); 68 (Indianapolis Museum of Art at Newfields/Jane Wacker Memorial Fund); 80, 117 (Granger); 88 left (Private Collection/Archives Charmet); 107 right (Private Collection); 132 left (© George Hoyningen-Huene); 140, 153 (Bibliotheque des Arts Decoratifs/Archives Charmet); 144 (Lebrecht History); 149 above (© Julien Faure/Leextra via Leemage)

© Carla Coulson: 77

Collection Jean-Charles Varennes: 23

© Connaissance des Arts: 120 below

Dallas Museum of Art, The Wendy and Emery Reves Collection: 119, 120 above

Getty Images: Cover, 74, 84, 128, 142 right (Boris Lipnitzki); 2 (Cecil Beaton); 4, 83 (Douglas Kirkland); 10, 174-175 (Patrick Aventurier); 12 (Jarry/Tripelon); 18, 20 (LL); 28, 53, 58, 59 (Heritage Images); 40-41 (Jerome_Correia); 42, 43, 45 (Apic); 48, 161 (Carl Oscar August Erickson); 56 (Martial Colomb); 63, 86, 90, 97, 103, 112, (Hulton Archive); 67 left (George Hoyningen-Huene); 67 right, 68 above right, 68 below left, 131 (Edward Steichen); 68 below right (Chicago History Museum); 70-71 (Westend61); 72 (Unknown/Conde Nast Collection); 76 (Kammerman); 78-79, 154 (Robert Doisnau); 94-95 (Ullstein Bild Dtl); 102 (Robert Patterson); 107 left (George Sheeler); 114-115 (© Allard Schager); 122, 134 Time Life Pictures; 132 right (Albert Harlingue); 136, 143 left (Keystone France); 137 (Universal History Archive); 156 (Jacques Sierpinski); 158 (Jacques Boucher); 162 (Horst P Horst); 165, 167 (Henry Clarke); 168 left (Paul Schutzer); 168 right (Adoc-photos); 170 (Giancarlo Botti); 173 (Erling Mandelmann); 179 (Bettmann); 181 (Photo 12); 182 (Patrice Habans)

© The Metropolitan Museum of Art/Art Resource/Scala Archives, Florence: 15, 127 right, 178

© Patrick Monchicourt (morio60 / Flickr): 24

Images © National Museums Scotland: 138, 139

© Nicolas Anetson: 65

© Ohio State University Historic Costume & Textiles Collection: 127 left

Rex Features: 8, 27, 37, 146, 150 (Granger/ Shutterstock); 126 (Peter Seyfferth/ imageBROKER/Shutterstock); 149 below (Romuald Meigneux/Sipa/Shutterstock); 157 (Shutterstock)

© Darren Robertson: 101

Photo Roger Schall © Collection Schall: 108, 116, 123

© Shutterstock: 36 (Elena Dijour); 177 (Catarina Belova)

© Caroline Young: 30, 167

© John Young: 13, 14

Index

Acknowledgements

This book has been an absolute joy to write, as I explored the places that meant so much to Coco Chanel. I'd like to give special thanks to Iain Cram at Bell Ingram for generously allowing me to explore Rosehall House, to Lisa Mason at National Museums Scotland for her assistance in showcasing their Chanel pieces, to Dallas Museum of Art for their information on La Pausa, to Sylvie Roy and Nathalie Gourseau at The Palais Galliera, Paris, and Jean-Jaccques Eggler at Ville de Lausanne archives.

I would also like to give heartfelt thanks to Nicki Davis at White Lion for overseeing this fascinating project, Charlotte Frost who has been an amazing editor, and Paileen Currie for her beautiful book design, which has brought Chanel's journey to life.

Brimming with creative inspiration, how-to projects and useful information to enrich your everyday life, Quarto Knows is a favourite destination for those pursuing their interests and passions. Visit our site and dig deeper with our books into your area of interest: Quarto Creates, Quarto Cooks, Quarto Homes, Quarto Lives, Quarto Drives, Quarto Explores, Quarto Gifts, or Quarto Kids.

First published in 2019 by White Lion Publishing,
an imprint of The Quarto Group.
The Old Brewery, 6 Blundell Street
London, N7 9BH,
United Kingdom
T (0)20 7700 6700
www.QuartoKnows.com

Text © 2019 Caroline Young
© 2019 Quarto Publishing plc

A catalogue record for this book is available from the British Library.

ISBN 978 0 71124 034 6
Ebook ISBN 978 0 71124 706 2

10 9 8 7 6 5 4 3 2 1

Printed in China